STRIKE By NAME

One Man's Part in the 1984-5 Miners' Strike

by Norman Strike

To my children, Jennifer, Sasha and Tim
and to all the striking miners and their
families who lasted the distance

Strike by Name: One Man's Part in the 1984-5 Miners' Strike

Copyright © Norman Strike, 2009
Published by Bookmarks, 2009
www.bookmarks.uk.com

ISBN: 9781905192557

Design by Adam Di Chiara
Cover photograph by John Sturrock/Network Photographers
Printed by Mixam Press

6	Preface
8	Introduction
11	Early Days
25	Whoopee
35	Socialism & Cash
45	Zulu, Zulu, Zulu
49	Flying Squad
71	Frustration
79	Orgreave
87	Police & Thieves
93	Fighting Thatcher
107	Prison Notes
117	Keep On Keepin' On
139	Justice
141	1980 Fuckin' 5
153	Chronology
156	Glossary

PREFACE

by Mike Simons

The 1984-85 miners' strike was the longest, most bitter national strike in British working class history. For 12 months the miners fought an unprecedented battle to defend their jobs and communities against the full might of the government and ruling class.

The miners withstood savage police brutality, travesties of justice in the courts, poverty, hunger and a sustained onslaught by the media, yet they held firm. Almost 10,000 miners were arrested during the strike. More than 180 miners spent time in jail and 700 were sacked in its aftermath.

Welfare and social services agencies were turned into a weapon by Margaret Thatcher's Tory government, denying miners and their families the benefits they were entitled to, in a bid to starve them back to work.

Rather than surrender, the mining communities transformed themselves. Men and women joined picket lines, travelled the country speaking at meetings to raise funds and organised food kitchens.

This diary brings that process to life. Norman Strike's memoir is a raw, day-by-day, blow-by-blow account of a year that changed Britain for ever. These pages spell out the anger and frustration, the hopes and fears of a young activist realising the enormity of the battle the miners were forced to fight.

They show Norman's changing perception of individuals and organisations: trade unions, socialist organisations, politicians, government and the police.

It pulls no punches. It commits to paper the feelings of the thousands of young militants on the front line of the strike, as the fight ebbed and flowed. It lambasts individuals and organisations, and Norman's thoughts are reproduced unedited, to capture the flavour of the times. Some of his judgements may seem harsh, though looking back 25 years, most stand the test of time. Others, as the diary makes clear, were revised as the strike went on.

Above all, this very personal account is a timely reminder of the issues around which the strike was fought: That people come before profit, that workers don't have to bow down to market forces, that solidarity can overcome isolation and fear, and that ordinary people can change themselves and their communities when they unite together.

Today the God of free market capitalism and globalisation—worshiped by both Tories and Labour—and at the heart of the miners' strike, stands utterly exposed. That is why the publication of this diary today is so timely. These pages are an inspiration for a new generation to take up the trade union and socialist fight for a better world.

Mike Simons is the author of
Striking Back: Photographs of the Great Miners' Strike 1984-85

INTRODUCTION

It was the fight of our lives. The way we stood up for what we believed in took everyone by surprise. Most people thought our strike would all be over and lost in weeks, optimists thought a few months, but no one, especially the activists, thought it would last a year.

The Tories won the battle but they didn't win the war. Some lost their lives in the fight, others their freedom. Marriages broke up, debts mounted up and homes were lost. Yet despite everything the state could throw against us, the majority of us saw the strike out without scabbing and betraying our class. I will always be proud of the part I played, and if I had my time over I would do it all again.

I was born in South Shields into a working class family. My dad was a train driver and my mam worked as a bar maid. We lived in a council house and I went to a secondary modern school. I left at 15 with no qualifications at all and, stupidly, joined the army. A bad move because I was always in trouble at school for questioning authority and this continued in my short spell of military service.

At 17 I became an apprentice miner at Westoe Colliery and hated it. I went down the pit at 18, but like a lot of my generation became involved in the drug scene. The two things didn't match up and I packed the pit in and spent a few years in a drug induced haze. I was one of the lucky ones and didn't follow my friends into heroin addiction and an early grave.

I met Kath in 1972 and we got married, forcing me to become more responsible and less selfish. Jennifer was born in 1972, and Sasha in 1974, both miners' strike years so at least those power cuts helped to create more than just Tory defeats.

I worked for a couple of years first for British Steel at the Jarrow Rolling Mill, then as a bus conductor, both dead end jobs with poor wages so in 1976 I bit the bullet and became a miner again to earn better money.

I hated it, working under the North Sea in bad conditions but was forced to continue because I had a young family to fend for. I became a coal face worker in the late seventies after doing my time and working my way up. I had better wages but still the same poor working conditions. The only thing that made it bearable was the men I worked alongside, great people, salt of the earth.

At the start of the eighties I became interested in the union and entered an annual writing competition where the prize was a week at Stirling University.

In 1981 I was one of the runners up and only got a weekend away at Whitby, but in 1982 and 1983 I was one of the winners and spent time in Scotland. It was here I first met Arthur Scargill and became very interested in left wing politics, and stood for the National Union of Mineworkers' Lodge Committee.

I was defeated by seven votes but got on the Committee because someone died. However, it only lasted a few months, enough to show me it wasn't really for me. I entered another writing competition, and wrote a short story that won second place.

Encouraged, I enrolled on an Open University course, 'The 19th Century Novel and its Legacy' and used to read the novels I had to study down the pit as I travelled in the 'manset', a 'train' that carried the miners into the seams about seven miles from the shaft. I'd sit there and read Jane Austen, Dickens, Turgenev, Tolstoy, and my favourite, *Germinal* by Zola. Then came the strike and everything changed.

I've always kept a diary, though not usually as detailed as the one I kept during the strike. I just sensed that this strike was going to be special in some way, and as it progressed that became clearer. I wanted to have something to show my daughters when they grew up and started to ask questions about that year, so I wrote everything down. I'm glad I did. They were my thoughts of the time, written in the heat of the struggle.

That year changed my life forever. I went from being a happily married husband and father with no debt and a steady job, to a single man who was homeless and riddled with debt. But after a short period of struggle I got my life back on track and started afresh.

There were at least half a dozen lads who lost their lives and dozens of others who suffered serious injuries. Lots of lads were jailed, hundreds of marriages ended, and scabs divided families. Whole communities were decimated, pits were closed and jobs were lost. I was lucky and escaped, got an education and transformed my life for the better. The same positive thing happened for lots of men and women, and society is the better for it.

I'm still good friends with Kath and she has been worried she will come across as anti-strike and unsupportive to people reading this diary. She wasn't either of those things and has encouraged me to publish the diary, warts and all.

What happened to us happened to thousands of others, and at least we came out of the whole tumultuous year as good friends, eventually. The world turned upside down, but we have put it back and are better people for the experiences we went through 25 years ago.

Norman Strike, June 2009

EARLY DAYS

Saturday March 10th, 1984
This morning I attended a packed out meeting in Sunderland which was addressed by NUM President Arthur Scargill. Predictably he started by making lots of uncomplimentary comments about Ian MacGregor, the government's 'hatchet man', and warned that it is now or never as far as fighting the threat of pit closures goes. He urged us to come out now in support of men in Yorkshire and Scotland who are already on strike to fight the plans to close 5 pits immediately, with another 65 to follow if we don't stand up now. He made it sound like Custer's Last Stand but I still agree with his views. Rhetoric is his forte, and because I've heard him speak quite a lot over the past few years he does tend to sound repetitive.

One point of criticism I would make is that he attacked the 'leeches of the capitalist media' who were there in force. If he hates them so much why doesn't he just ban them from his meetings? I suspect it's because his ego enjoys the attention, but that doesn't take away from he fact that he's the best union leader we have. He's right when he says that pits are being deliberately starved of investment and are fobbed off with secondhand machinery. It's happening at my pit, Westoe Colliery in South Shields, where we lost £3m last year despite producing over a million tons of coal.

Anyway, he ended with, 'Get off your knees and fight like men to save your jobs and communities!' He got a tremendous ovation from the packed hall, and if that's anything to go by then we'll vote for strike at our Lodge meeting tomorrow morning at 11am. I will, of course, be voting for strike. How could I do anything else with a surname like mine!

Sunday March 11th, 1984
At a mass meeting held at the Armstrong Hall, South Shields, this morning over 1,000 men voted to come out on strike in protest against the pit closures announced by the NCB. It was the best attended Lodge meeting

I have ever been to and everyone present was given the opportunity to air their views, some brave men actually speaking against the strike. I of course spoke in support before the Lodge Secretary summed up the main events that have led to today's vote. He reminded us of what MacGregor had done to British Steel and the thousands of jobs lost in Consett and Jarrow.

After a lengthy debate someone proposed a rider to the main motion asking the National Executive to hold a national ballot and this was passed, though a sizeable minority of us were against a national ballot. To be honest I don't want one because I feel we would lose it, and I feel the issue is too important to be decided by an ageing workforce who don't have as much to lose as us younger men. All we'll have facing us is a life on the dole if Thatcher gets her way because she won't stop at 5 pits, more like 70! Anyway, Scargill is right when he says it isn't our job to sell, it belongs to future generations. The strike vote was overwhelming, with only 20 men voting no, so we're out as from now.

At Westoe we have already had a taste of the new, no listen NCB. Back in September the new manager at Westoe decided everyone was going to do the 10pm night shift on a rota system, whereas it had always been done by men who liked doing the night shift. He just had posters put up around the pit stating the new arrangement would start on September 26th and refused to negotiate with the union. He also threatened to cut jobs if we refused to comply. So we had a big union meeting and voted to strike. We were undermined by the mechanics' union who refused to join us because their members already had to work night shift. I could understand that but not their unions advice to their members to cross our picket lines. It caused a lot of aggro, especially when one idiot drove his car at high speed through our line. The police turned out in force as things got nasty and we had a lot of pushing and shoving. We tried to make it light hearted by chanting, 'Zulu, Zulu, Zulu', and trying different formations to charge into the police. The film had just been on the telly so it was fresh in our minds. We won the strike after just over a week out and the manager withdrew his demands but I doubt it will be that easy this time.

Monday March 12th, 1984

I should have been getting up at 2.30am to get ready for the 4am shift. Instead I got a lie in until 5.30am but when I looked out of the bedroom window at the rain lashing down outside I was tempted to get back into bed. I didn't, and instead got dressed in warm clothes, had a mug of coffee, then picked up my home made placard that read, 'Fight for Coal, Keep Miners Off the Dole'. Totally unoriginal but the best I could come up with late last night. I was off to Boldon Colliery where a whale shaped mound of coal is being stockpiled. A year ago it had been a working pit but is now just a place to store a mountain of coal. That's why I was going, to try and stop lorries moving the coal.

I arrived at just before six and was supposed to meet up with John McIvor, who has a nice warm car we were supposed to sit in. He still wasn't there an hour later and I was bloody soaked. I cursed him and was ready to pack it in when a lorry roared up to the entrance, snapping me out of my apathy.

I approached the driver's window and bent my neck backwards to speak up to him. I told him I was an official NUM picket and that in the interests of solidarity he should go no further. The driver's response was to open his door and jump down, which gave me a bit of a shock, but I was on my guard and ready for anything. He said, 'Ya bloody jokin' aren't y' son. Are you all there is? Not much of a picket line, is it?' He was a big bloke with hamshank forearms and he sounded aggressive but I replied,' It only takes one man to form a picket and I'm it. Other lads will be getting here soon.' The last bit was a lie but I didn't want him to think I was on my own. He mumbled something about the bloody miners not supporting him when he was on strike and then climbed back into his lorry. I was really chuffed when he turned his lorry round and drove off, stopping quickly to tell the other drivers arriving what was happening, and then they drove off as well. I couldn't believe it! I had stopped 7 lorries on my own and if everyone treats our picket lines with the same respect the strike will be over in weeks.

At a quarter to nine Kath turned up to give me a flask of coffee and a dry coat. She was in our first car, an L reg Hillman Imp. She was on her way to work, and the fact she has a job will make life a bit easier for us, even though she only earns about £50 a week. Kath isn't too impressed with the strike because for the first time in our married life we are getting a few of life's luxuries, like the car and a new washing machine, and she is hoping we'll get back to work soon. I'm not at all optimistic about that because I don't think Thatcher has provoked this strike to give in quickly. Anyway, I'm just pleased to be out in the fresh air and not stuck down the pit in the dust and dirt.

I got Kath to give me a lift to the pit because I was keen to let everyone know what had happened. I was pleased to hear the strike is solid at Westoe, with only a few Deputies being allowed in for safety reasons, and the office workers so they could sort out our wages and coal deliveries to retired miners. I spoke to a union official to get a rota sorted out for picketing at Boldon and he introduced me to a female reporter from *Newcastle Evening Chronicle*. She was very interested in my account of Boldon, even more when she heard my name. Like Scargill, my ego took over and I chatted to her and had my photo taken. I got my just deserts when the paper came out tonight and the story was on the front page under a small headline that read 'Strike By Name' and gave the impression I was a very experienced striker. I shall have to be more careful in the future if I have any more dealings with the media.

News of the strike is not too good, with Northumberland still working, as well as a few pits in Durham. If they won't fall into line we'll have to picket them out. Mind you, so far it's the same lads on the picket line who were there in September and we'll need more than that if we want to win this one.

Tuesday March 13th, 1984

I was up and out of bed at 2.30am this morning so that I could walk the 5 miles to the pit to get there in time for the first shift due at 3.30am. Westoe's workforce is a mixture of 'Sanddancers', men from the coastal areas, and 'Hillbillies', those lads bussed in from the inland pitless villages of County Durham. Some of the 'Hillbillies' have been at over 5 pits that have been closed, and there are a lot of veterans from the '72 and '74 strikes.

Wednesday March 14th, 1984

From the reports I've heard from the lads who were at Dawdon last night it was a successful night and the Dawdon men have joined the strike. The news on Metro Radio put it rather differently, calling the pickets 'animals and hooligans'. Whatever, it's the result that counts and Durham is a step nearer being 100% solid. Apparently the Westoe lads did themselves proud, spurring on what had been a passive picket with their war cry of 'Zulu'. There was some violence, with a car being given a good shaking until the driver saw sense and turned round and left. A few bottles were smashed but there were no arrests.

This morning I had a bit of a lie in and didn't get to the pit until 8.30, just in time to shout at management as they crossed our picket lines in posh cars. A lad told me a coach was leaving at nine to go up to Northumberland to try and picket them out. They have voted overwhelmingly to stay at work, despite the fact that their pits are amongst the most likely to be shut by MacGregor. It was up to us to make them see sense and change their minds.

There were only about thirty of us on the coach which had room for 55 so we were a bit disappointed, especially as a lot of the lads had been at Dawdon last night and had taken the trouble to turn up for this. We had the dubious privilege of having five Lodge officials with us, including Billy Jerry, the Treasurer, but none of them had any ideas about which pit to picket. I suggested Ellington because that's where MacGregor became the 'fall guy' the other week. Mind you, I had no idea where Ellington was other than it was somewhere near Blyth, and I didn't know where that was either! Fortunately for us the driver did and we arrived at 9.30 just in time to catch the main shift of the day going down at ten. We told the driver to come back for us at twelve and then set the Lodge banner up at the main entrance.

It was bloody freezing cold with a bitterly cold wind blowing in from the North Sea, just like at Westoe, and we stamped up and down and rubbed our hands together in a futile attempt to get warm. The pit manager showed up and ordered us to get off Coal Board property. We noisily refused and he stormed off to get the police to remove us. A few of the lads needed to take a piss but when they tried to go into the pit management magically appeared and stopped them. This only riled us up the more and the lads pissed against the wall, much to the disgust of management, but when you gotta go you gotta go!

Just as we were starting to get bored a delivery van turned up. We had a quick word with the driver and asked him not to cross our picket line. We were delighted when he agreed and turned round and drove off. We all applauded his solidarity noisily, even more when two local union officials turned up looking grim. They told us to leave because they had taken a democratic decision and that we should respect that. One of our union officials told them that as trade unionists they should respect our right to picket and not to cross our picket line. The two of them stormed off to report to their members waiting in the pit canteen who had arrived before us.

Shortly afterwards a coach arrived and we lined up across the entrance to stop it so we could appeal to the men to join us. A union official showed up and told the men that an emergency meeting was being held in the pit canteen to discuss what to do about our picket. We agreed to let the men through but urged them to back us, stressing the need for unity in the face of pit closures. I was disgusted when one of the men told me they had voted 10 to 1 against the strike but not that surprised when I learned they were also amongst the highest paid miners in the country because of high bonus payments. This just proves how divisive the Incentive Scheme is in rewarding men who work in good conditions with higher wages than those of us who struggle in poor ones, and it was a bloody Labour government who brought it in!

The two union officials returned to make a final attempt to get us to leave. One of them said, 'Thatcher's laughing her head off at this, mind. You lot will close the pits by being on strike!' His mate added, 'If we stay at work it'll put pressure on the National Executive to hold a ballot. We want a ballot!' We responded by telling them that we had voted with our feet, and anyway we were in line with the Delegate Conference decision to strike if any pit was closed on economic grounds. The two of them left in a huff to attend their meeting.

As we waited a TV crew from Tyne Tees Television showed up and tried to ask questions in a fairly aggressive manner. Our union official was brilliant and refused to rise to the bait but put our case across well. Keith Smoult ended the interview by nipping the reporter's arse, with him complaining loudly about being 'goosed'. This gave us all a welcome laugh until an angry woman turned up and started to shout at us to 'bugger off back where you come from!' She told the eager TV crew that her man wanted to work. We put our bodies and placards in front of the camera to shut her up. I felt sorry for the husband!

The two union officials returned looking very glum and told us the men of Ellington had voted to join the strike and from now on would picket their own pit. We cheered loudly, especially when we were allowed into the pit canteen to get a hot drink. We asked the Treasurer for some funds and he responded by buying 7 sausage rolls! It was just like Jesus with the bread and fishes.

We returned to Westoe in high spirits, immensely proud that the 'Zulu pickets' had closed the largest pit in Northumberland with no hint of violence. The local television news reported that 'men from Westoe Colliery brought the NCB's showpiece pit, Ellington, to a standstill with a peaceful and good humoured picket, unlike the ugly and disgraceful scenes at Dawdon last night'. That gave me a laugh because it was mostly the same men!

The news is generally good, with Yorkshire pickets having a lot of success in Notts, and there are not many pits still working. It's looking good.

Thursday March 15th, 1984

Did the picket at Westoe for a few hours but nothing happened; we just stood about and talked about the strike. I went round to visit a mate of mine, and fellow miner, Dave Farham. He is an inspirational man who, despite suffering from MS, does as much as he can to support the strike. It was nice to sit in front of his coal fire and have a cup of coffee. I started to tell him about yesterday's events but he already knew because he only lives a few hundred yards from the picket line. Anyway, when I took a pause for breath he told me that he had been invited to speak at a student meeting in Newcastle and would I go with him for moral support? I agreed because my daughters were at school and Kath was at work so I had the day to myself. Phil Turner, Dave's friend, who is a student at Newcastle Poly, turned up and we all caught the bus to Newcastle.

On the way Phil told me he was a member of the Socialist Workers Party and that immediately put me on my guard because since Monday all kinds of political activists had begun to show up–SWP, WRP, CP and *Militant*. As a member of the Labour Party I tended to veer towards the latter and they had warned me that the SWP were extremists. Nevertheless I liked Phil straightaway and he was very open about his beliefs, which I also liked. He told us we were going to a General Meeting of the Students Union which had been called to discuss a motion that would give full support to the NUM and allow us to use their facilities. Phil asked if Dave and me would speak in support of the motion and we agreed, though he warned that there might not be enough people present to have a quorum. Dave and me weren't worried about that because at least we would get the chance to raise awareness of the strike.

The crowded room we saw when we arrived gave us both a panic attack and we were all for going straight back home but when we were led to a table full of students we calmed down a bit. I stupidly thought that that these were the students we were going to talk to but Phil soon corrected that when he led us up onto a stage and we nervously sat down in front of about 500 noisy students. I drew the short straw and was asked to speak first. My legs were shaking as I stood up and spoke about why we were on strike and why it was vital for us to win. I got a good round of applause. Dave came forward to speak but was forced to wait while a Tory student spoke against the motion, making lots of provocative remarks about miners, and Scargill in particular.

Dave was brilliant! Not only did he answer the Tory criticisms but he also attacked the Thatcher government's stated goal of smashing the unions. He warned the students that the Tories would force students to pay for their own education if they were allowed to beat us. He got a well deserved standing ovation and everyone felt confident that the motion would be carried.

The last speaker was a fat, posh Tory who was so right wing he made Thatcher seem like a communist! He tried to convince the meeting that miners were a highly paid group of workers, and that it was only a small group of left wing agitators, led by Scargill, who were against the closure of uneconomic pits. At the mention of wages Dave leapt to his feet and offered to show his last payslip for the princely sum of £67 for a 42 hour week! Predictably the Tory refused to look at it, despite a noisy majority of students' calling for him to, 'Read it out! Read it out!' and the rest of his speech was drowned out by the chant.

A vote was called for and the Tories made constant interruptions to try and prevent a vote being taken. The bastards even set off the fire alarm but to the students' great credit the vote was taken and the motion passed. Phil gave us £23 from a collection and we both felt very humble that students, not the richest members of society, could still be generous. It was a very memorable day.

The media are generally speaking against the strike and are supporting the miners in Notts who are refusing to come out, despite heavy picketing from Yorkshire. We need to go down there and support them.

Sunday March 18th, 1984

Tragically a young Yorkshire miner, David Jones, was killed at Ollerton Colliery in Notts the other day and the Tories are calling for an end to all picketing. Fuck them! We need to step up the picketing so the lad's death isn't totally in vain, and get those scabby bastards out!

A small group of us at Westoe are growing increasingly disillusioned with our Lodge officials because they seem totally disinterested in organising picketing. So we have set up our own unofficial strike committee to raise funds and organise men to go where they are needed. The Lodge have totally refused to send men down to Notts, even though we are 100% solid. I don't know how they can be so short sighted.

Militant have promised to help us raise funds in the shipyards and to put us in touch with other miners in our area who want to fight. Hopefully we can show our stupid officials that we are more than capable of organising ourselves. If we wait for them to take the lead the strike will be lost!

Tuesday March 20th, 1984

This morning a couple of us went over to Swan Hunter's shipyards in Wallsend to try and collect some money with some SWP members. I was a bit surprised at the generally negative attitude of the men going into the shipyard. One man said he was going to lose his job anyway, so why should he support us? Despite this we still managed to collect £46 which I hope will help finance pickets to go down to Notts. We made sure that all those contributing knew what the money would be used for, and that we were working independently of our Lodge. We did this so no one could accuse us of collecting for our own pockets. We bought a cash book and entered every penny we'd collected and had it signed by witnesses for the same reason.

The SWP members we collected with made no attempt to recruit us, unlike *Militant*, and when I asked why they said I should make up my own mind. They also suggested I should attend one of their meetings, and perhaps I will because they seem like genuine people.

The police presence in Notts has been stepped up dramatically and the Yorkshire pickets are being stopped from even entering the county! The scabs in Notts have made it clear they have no intention of entering the strike unless a national ballot is held. Their union leaders have told them that it is alright for them to cross picket lines because the strike is 'unofficial'. This is a disgusting betrayal of basic trade union principles. If the picket line isn't respected they will play straight into the hands of Thatcher!

Thursday March 22nd, 1984

John McIvor picked me up at 6.30am to go to the Whitburn Workshops because we had heard that COSA staff are still working. Whitburn is halfway between South Shields and Sunderland on the coast and was the site of one of the most militant pits in the North East before its closure in the sixties. A lot of the men who used to work at Whitburn Colliery now work at Westoe and are very proud of their militant past. They believe the pit was closed because of its militancy because there was plenty of coal left there. All that remains now is a few rows of colliery houses and a waste heap. The NCB now use part of the site for offices and workshops.

We were surprised by the size of the picket when we arrived, about 70 men, mostly from Wearmouth Colliery. We parked the car in a nearby street and then joined the 6 Westoe men present. They asked where the rest of the Westoe pickets were. I told them they were standing outside Westoe doing nothing. A Wearmouth lad asked the same question, only he used more colourful language. We agreed that our lads should be here but that we have nothing to do with organising and had just come along on our own initiative.

Talking with the Wearmouth lads has made us realise just how bad our own officials are. Not only do the Wearmouth lads have their own bus to transport pickets, but they also have a Strike HQ where pickets can get a hot meal when they return from picketing. This isn't that much of a surprise because their officials are predominantly left wing so they were prepared for the strike before it happened. That's why they invited Scargill to come and speak the other week.

This morning's picket was a partial success, with the mechanics from the workshops agreeing to join the strike. The mostly female COSA members refused to join us, and after a bit of pushing they were escorted in by the police. John and I returned to the pit where the last payslips were being handed out. I was determined to confront our Lodge officials and ask them to arrange for men to be sent to Whitburn in the morning to support the Wearmouth lads.

In the pit yard a long snaking queue had formed to wait for the pay office to open at nine. I spotted Walter Slater, the Lodge Secretary, and John Chapman, the Chairman, talking to some lads so I went to tell them about Whitburn. When I'd finished telling them what was happening their attitude really riled me. They said that Whitburn had nothing to do with them, and if Wearmouth chose to send pickets then that was their business. I said that scabbing was every miner's business and that if we didn't nip it in the bud it would spread. Slater got really angry at this and asked me what experience I had of being on strike, giving the answer himself and calling me a 'red troublemaker'. He added that the Westoe men had shown what they thought of my abilities at the last elections by not voting for me! This was true but it doesn't mean that what I said was any less true. Anger then got the better of me and I shouted that it was a disgrace we weren't supporting the Wearmouth lads, and how could they be so well organised and we weren't! He replied that when I was doing his job I could do what I liked, but as I wasn't, and he was, then he would not be responsible for 'wasting Lodge money'. I exploded at this and called him a 'stupid bastard!' I also said he wouldn't have a Lodge to be Secretary of if we lost the strike. I stormed off, getting even more 'red' taunts from men waiting in the queue. What really pissed me off was that a few of the 'unofficial strike committee' were present and said nothing to support me. Very disappointing.

Outside the pit gates I met Margaret Reavey, a *Militant* supporter, and she took me to a nearby pub and let me vent my anger a bit. She also introduced me to some lads from the APEX union who gave me a cheque for £25 made out to the union. We had a good discussion about the strike and she invited me to go to Sheffield on Saturday for the Broad Left Organising Committee Conference. I've been down to Broad Left miners' meetings in Easington so I agreed to go, especially as they are paying. John is going as well so at least I'll have someone to talk to if it all gets boring.

Kath is NOT pleased about me going to Sheffield because Saturday is the one day we get to spend some time together and have a night out. I told her she'd better get used to it because winning this strike is my top priority, and because I've been a very vocal supporter of Scargill since before he was elected President, I can't now take a back seat and let others do the fighting. She went to bed in a huff!

Friday March 23rd, 1984

David Jones, the picket killed in Notts, was buried this morning. His funeral was attended by over 4,000 people from every coalfield in the country. I only saw it on the TV news because no one bothered to tell me a coach was going from Westoe.

Instead I attended a meeting in Newcastle at which Ken Livingstone was speaking. He spoke well and voiced his support for the NUM. It's only a pity he couldn't put his money where his big mouth is because he only put £3 in the bucket I stuck in front of him. A tiny amount when you think about what he must earn in a year! Tight bastard! Anyway, we still managed to collect £33.09p, not bad seeing as it was collected outside Newcastle Poly. As usual we counted it in front of witnesses and got them to sign the cash book.

I've just spoken to one of the lads on the phone and he told me how the Westoe coach had been stopped by the police on the A1, just outside Durham. The police said they had reason to believe that the men were about to commit a breach of the peace by engaging in unlawful picketing. This was plainly a load of bollocks because the lads were dressed in suits and ties, hardly picketing gear for a cold March morning! The police made the lads get off the coach while they searched it. One constable, of normal police intelligence, asked what the black case lying down the aisle of the coach was? A lad shouted, 'It's a bloody bazooka!' The PC responded by ordering that the case be removed from the coach so it could be searched! Incredible, and yet another example of the misuse of police powers, just like the other week when Kent miners were stopped from going through the Dartford Tunnel. Our lads were plainly on their way to a funeral, which the police must have known, so the only conclusion is they are trying to harass and provoke us! The driver was told to drive the coach back to Shields and the lads weren't allowed to attend the funeral. Disgraceful!

An official complaint has been made but I doubt anything will come of it. I've also heard that the Lodge had a lot of trouble hiring a coach because local bus companies have been warned by police not to hire vehicles to the NUM. This is another outrageous abuse of police powers and a threat to our ability to travel to picket lines. They won't stop us though because we can use cars, if the bloody Lodge will supply petrol money. It's about time they started to use some of the funds they must've built up since 1974!

Saturday March 24th, 1984

I left the house at 6.30am and the rain was lashing down. It's still lashing down now as I write this at 11.30pm! Anyway I made my way up to Newcastle and arrived soaking wet at around 7.30am. I grabbed a coffee to warm up and met with Margaret and a couple of other people. The coach arrived shortly afterwards and we piled on, the inside soon resembling a sauna as we all steamed away in the warm. The passengers were mainly *Militant* supporters, with a few SWP members as well. They got straight on with the job of selling their paper *Socialist Worker* and I bought one to see what news they had about the strike.

I sat next to a lass called Pat who is an SWP member and works at Newcastle Poly. We chatted about the strike and she told me she's been down to Westoe a few times. She gave me £10 she had collected and talked about the SWP but she was equally talkative about the shortcomings of the Labour Party, especially Tony Benn and his role in pushing through the hated Incentive Scheme when he was Energy Secretary in the last Labour government. I agreed with most of what she had to say but remained suspicious of her motives.

The rain was still pissing down when we arrived in Sheffield so we sprinted across the road and into the University where a long queue was waiting to register for the Conference. I was pleased to see Keith Smoult because it would be good to have someone from Westoe to talk to, and because he is a member of the Young Socialists he already knew a lot of people there, including Geoff, the head *Militant* man, who took us into the canteen whilst he sorted out tickets.

It seemed that the miners were the stars of the moment because when we got into the main hall all the front rows were filled with NUM members. I got a load of union badges to stick on my flat cap. The hall was packed with people from every union, some of which I'd never even heard of! All the speakers in the morning session made comforting noises about supporting us miners but seemed to me to be more concerned with electing left wing union leaders and politicians into various obscure roles. A collection was taken which raised over £2,000, half to go to the NUM, the other to the Broad Left. A group of people, who I later learned were all SWP members, complained and said all the money should go to the miners. A lively debate followed but the motion was defeated, much to my disappointment because I thought they were right.

At lunchtime I was persuaded to attend a fringe meeting to be addressed by someone called Tony Cliff which would be about the strike. It was held in a small room but it was packed, and to be honest, when I first saw and heard the guy I thought to myself, who the bloody hell is this! He was an old guy, short and stocky, with wiry grey hair sticking out from either side of his head, and wearing glasses. He had a strong foreign accent which I found hard to understand at first. However, once I was tuned in I found myself agreeing with almost everything he said. He wasn't like other speakers I had heard because he openly criticised Scargill and the NUM leadership saying they were tactically naïve! He drew comparisons between the '72 and '74 strikes and now, saying we couldn't win this one just by closing down power stations, mainly because of the time of year but also because we would not get support from other trade unionists unless we began campaigning for support now amongst the rank and file. He warned that the other trade union leaders would do to us what they had done to the NGA at Warrington and the people at GCHQ. They would stab us in the back and leave us to fight on our own. He said our only hope was to appeal to workers directly by going to their meetings and explaining exactly what the strike was about. He got a tremendous round of applause and I for one thought what he had to say made sense, even if it did depress me a bit!

A Yorkshire miner spoke next and made an appeal for money to send pickets into Notts. He spoke with passion and got a great round of applause. He also got £644, a sum that surprised me because I have never gotten into three figures. One thing I will say is the SWP are certainly a party of action!

As I headed back to the main hall I met a lad called Yunus from Newcastle who I'd seen down at Westoe a few times. He said I should collect money outside instead of listening to hot air inside! I was a bit dubious but he went and got me a bucket covered in 'Support the miners' stickers. He assured me it was OK but a steward disagreed. Yunus had a word with an official and I was given permission to stay, so I did.

I was soon joined by some Yorkshire miners who were a bit cool towards me at first but after 20 minutes or so we were getting along like a house on fire. One of the lads was called Ian and works at Silverwood Colliery. We got along particularly well, joining forces to verbally abuse a little runt of a man who more or less accused us of collecting the money for ourselves. Ian told me later he was a union official from Barnsley who didn't like the idea of anyone organising but elected officials. I told Ian about the officials at my pit and he said we should organise ourselves.

We spent the whole afternoon collecting, and such was our success that I was forced to put half of the bucket into a box at my feet because the bucket was so heavy! One big Scotsman tossed a quid into the bucket every time he came out to use the bog, which he did on a regular basis. He either had a weak bladder or had too much to drink, but whatever, I was impressed by his solidarity.

Geoff Price, the *Militant* guy, came to ask me why I wasn't listening to Tony Benn, and when I told him he wasn't happy and stormed off. He came back with some even bigger official from *Militant* who told me the SWP were a bunch of small time losers. I told him to piss off, so he did. Tosser!

When Keith and me counted up what I'd collected we were staggered to find the sum of £102.77p. We were over the moon but when we met some of the Wearmouth lads we decided to give them half, knowing it would be put to good use.

The journey home was spent talking politics, and one thing I am sure of and that is I have totally lost faith in the Labour Party. They need to get off the fence and start supporting us instead of trying to pander to the middle classes. They are a bloody disgrace to all those who went before them and who gave their blood to found trade unions.

Before we headed for home we bought fish and chips for the few lads on the Westoe picket line. After all, they are giving up their Saturday night and deserve a little treat. The bloody Lodge won't give them one!

Sunday March 25th, 1984

The Wearmouth Lodge Committee visited the Armstrong Hall this morning in an attempt to get some kind of co-ordination between our pits on picketing. Typically our officials gave them the cold shoulder and the Wearmouth lads stormed off muttering something about 'wankers'. Before they left one of them told me to be careful what I was doing because I am not very well thought of in the committee room. That comes as no surprise to me.

Surprisingly one of the same Lodge officials, Tommy Wilson, paid me a visit at home tonight to ask if I could give him some money so they could take an extra car down to Notts! I gave him £35 for petrol and got him to sign for it. I asked if I could go but he said I was doing an important job raising money and should continue doing that. In other words, piss off, you're not wanted! Depressing but not a big surprise.

WHOOPEE

Tuesday March 27th, 1984
I was on picket duty at Westoe this morning when Tommy and his Merry Men returned from their trip to Notts. The stories they had to tell were not designed to encourage anyone to follow in their wake. They told of a massive police presence and the subterfuge they had to use to cross the border into Notts. The police were turning back anyone who tried to get in by road, so Tommy and his lads had to trek across fields to reach a pit, with helicopters flying overhead shining down spotlights. When they did finally arrive at a pit, the police so outnumbered the pickets that they were totally powerless to do anything. They couldn't even shout 'Scab' because the police arrested anyone who did so!

The only positive thing they had to report was that the treatment they had received in the Barnsley Strike HQ had been excellent, with the Yorkshire lads doing all they could to make them feel welcome. Tommy gave the impression that it would be pointless for anyone to try and get into Notts, though he did add that everyone should see for themselves what was going on. I've seen the news coverage on telly but none of it has shown anything like what Tommy described. Anyway, I'll soon see for myself later today because I'm writing this in the Northern Labour College near Barnsley.

I travelled down here with nine other lads from Westoe in a van borrowed from the GMBU. Keith Smoult arranged it through his contacts in the Young Socialists. We picked the van up from Newcastle this evening and then went to the pit to get lads to join us. Brian Tate volunteered to drive, though after his driving on the way down I have strong reservations about his ability to get us anywhere safely! At one point he drove us straight over a roundabout!

The journey down was exciting, with everyone looking forward to seeing if what Tommy had said was true. With us we had Geordie Kane, one of the lads who had been with Tommy and who had just got back in the morning. He had volunteered to show us where to go because none of us had a clue. Geordie is like a father figure, laughing at our speculations about what would be in store, and saying, 'You'll see!' He also had a good laugh when Brian and me began singing an old hippie song, 'Feel Like I'm Fixin' to Die Rag' by Country Joe and the Fish, words altered slightly to suit the circumstances;

> "And it's one, two, three what are we fighting for?
> Don't ask me I don't give a damn
> Next stop is Nottingham
> And it's five, six, seven open up the pearly gates
> Well there aint no time to wonder why
> Whoopee we're all gonna die!"

The way Brian was driving that could well turn out to be true! Geordie said we were all mad, but if anyone was mad it was him because only a madman would risk the wrath of his wife by making a second journey without even telling her where he was going!

We arrived at Barnsley Strike HQ in the Junction Inn at midnight and were very surprised to find the place buzzing with activity, and even more surprised to have arrived there in one piece! We entered a smoke filled room upstairs which was full of lads, with telephones in constant use. The men had either just returned from, or were going into, Notts. I heard one lad tell of how his driver had been arrested for refusing to turn around at a police roadblock and the lads in the car had been stranded. They'd managed to hitch a lift back.

After hanging around for a while we were dealt with by a man whom I recognised straightaway. It was the 'little runt' from Sheffield who I'd had the row with. Fortunately he didn't recognise me and we were allocated accommodation here at the college. We were given a guide because Geordie couldn't remember the way. The 'guide' provided us with a very funny journey. He was a young lad in his teens, not very tall, and extremely pissed! He was riding a motor scooter, or trying to, and we were supposed to follow him in the van.

He wobbled off up the road, weaving from side to side, almost falling off on several occasions. We all laughed at his comical progress and took bets on how long it would be before he fell off. We didn't have long to wait. He tried to take a bend, fell off and went skidding across the road on his arse. We stopped quickly and piled out to see if he was alright. He never felt a thing, just staggered to his feet and grabbed his bike. He assured us he was fine but just to make sure we didn't run him over we got him to follow us because Geordie knew where to go.

So, here we are, two men to a room, with my roommate Dave still wandering around somewhere. The Wearmouth lads are also here but are going back in the morning. Unlike Tommy they've encouraged us to get into Notts, and have given us a pile of leaflets to give out to the scabs, in the unlikely event we get anywhere near them! It's an appeal from the Durham miners asking them to join the strike, and reminding them that no pit is safe from closure, wherever it is.

It's almost 3am so I'm going to get a few hours kip because we have to return to Barnsley at 7am, hopefully to make an attempt to get into Notts. I can't wait.

Wednesday March 28th, 1984

I was finally persuaded to get out of my comfortable bed at 6.30am, just in time to grab a cup of tepid black sugarless tea before heading out into the frosty morning air. The ground was white with a heavy frost and we had a bit of trouble getting the van started but it soon roared into life and we set off.

After taking a couple of wrong turnings we arrived at Strike HQ just after seven. The official on duty asked us if we were prepared to do some local picketing before trying to get into Notts and we all eagerly agreed, keen to do something useful to pay back the excellent hospitality we have received.

Our target was the aptly named town of Grimethorpe where we were to picket the NCB Area Offices. A lot of white collar workers from the APEX union were scabbing and we were going to try and stop them. We followed a car full of Yorkshire pickets to get there.

The picket was unsuccessful in terms of persuading the scabs to join the strike, but it did provide us with our first experience of the humour of a Yorkshire picket line. I have always held a kind of grudging respect towards the police, so the way those lads took the piss out of them came as a big surprise.

The main picket was at the top of a steep bank and there were about 50 lads present, and the roughly the same number of police. As we stood jeering at the scabs crossing our line, a lot of the pickets began to walk back down the hill. I asked one what was happening and he said, 'Follow me and tha'll see for thee sen.' We dutifully followed and speculated amongst ourselves what was going to happen. At the bottom all the lads turned to look back up the hill. We soon found out why as the police formed into ranks and began marching smartly down the hill. Just before they reached us the pickets formed into ranks and began goose-stepping back up the hill, laughing and jeering at the police as we passed. The police about turned and followed us, and again we about turned at the top and marched back down again, laughing at them. I was expecting the police to get angry and attack us but they didn't. They just followed us.

They must've been knackered in their heavy uniforms and pointy hats, titheads the Yorkshire lads called them. Anyway, it was funny and kept us amused at any rate.

Back at Strike HQ we were introduced to another car load of pickets who assured us they would get us into Notts, saying they'd never failed yet. Before we left I was given another £30 for petrol. Somehow I was looked upon as the leader so it was to me that a reporter and photographer from the *Morning Star* asked if we could give them a lift into Notts. No one had any objections so we set off, stopping at a local filling station to get fuel before heading for the M1. This didn't seem to us to be the most subtle route to take but the Yorkshire lads had been so confident that we weren't too worried.

Our confidence began to wilt a bit as we got further south, with every flyover we passed jammed full of police vans, bloody hundreds of them. Geordie kept repeating, 'You aint seen nothing yet!' The closer we got the more I had to agree because I have never seen so many police vehicles in my life! It was very intimidating and not a little scary.

We turned off the M1 at junction 29 and at the top of the slip road we were forced to take a diversion by police blockades. We were now certain that we would be stopped, especially as Geordie told us this is exactly what had happened to Tommy a few days before. Sure enough, as we approached a roundabout we were forced to go down a road that led to a police checkpoint. A policeman flagged us down and we could see about a dozen cars in front of us, their occupants lounging about on the grass verge.

The policeman approached Brian and said, 'Can I ask you where you are going sir?' Brian was at a loss what to say so he said we were going into Notts to hand out leaflets asking for support. With a huge grin on his face the copper said, 'I must warn you that if you proceed any further you will be arrested because I believe that if you proceed, a breach of the peace may ensue.' We all started shouting, saying we had no intention of breaching the peace and that they had no right to stop us. It was a bloody police state! A senior police officer came over and asked what the problem was, and when he heard our protests he said, 'Where have you lot come from then?' When Brian told him he said, 'You cheeky bastards! You've got some bloody nerve trying to get in, in broad daylight, in a bloody van!' He ordered us all out of the van except Brian, who had to give his details to a PC.

We stood on the grass verge, chatting to some lads from Cortonwood, one of the 5 pits that sparked the strike. They were delighted that Durham miners had joined the strike, and one of them admitted he was surprised because Durham has a reputation for being a moderate area. We told him we were surprised as well! The photographer asked us to pose for a photograph in front of a road sign that said 'Pleasley'. Brian was gutted because he loves having his photo taken and he was forced to miss out.

After a while the police ordered us all to get back into our vehicles. We did, but in a deliberately slow way to show a bit of defiance. According to the Yorkshire lads we were to be escorted back onto the M1, and some of them said they were going to block the M1 by driving slowly, as had happened yesterday. Brian refused to join in because he had been warned by the police that he would be arrested if he was caught driving in Notts again during the current dispute. We were escorted in convoy back onto the M1, with motorcycle outriders to make sure no one tried to escape. The blockade never materialised and we had a straightforward journey back to Barnsley.

Back at Strike HQ we were asked to return at 5pm and we had a brief discussion to decide whether it was worth it or not. We decided it was, and Jeff Mackins was appointed our new driver. We had some dinner back at the college and I had a few hours kip.

The staff at the college were fantastic, providing us with a huge parcel of sandwiches and fruit and an early tea. Well fed and provided for we set off back to Barnsley.

At Strike HQ we were given another £30 which we decided to share out for a little pocket money. I felt guilty about this but was outnumbered so reluctantly agreed. We were given a new guide, Malc, who worked at Grimethorpe and travelled in the van with us. He was a brilliant guide, not only taking us through three counties but also giving us a running commentary about places of interest along the way, including the birthplace of Arthur Scargill and the home of Jackie Charlton. We seemed to use every back road, track and minor road, and went in so many different directions none of us had a clue where we were, including Geordie. Incredibly we never saw any police until a car flew past us near our destination. We entered a housing estate and looked for a safe place to park, settling on a piece of waste land next to some garages. Thanks to Dekka we were all sticky and uncomfortable because he'd opened a bottle of coke and soaked everybody, and the inside of the van. Ian Wilburn looked like the 'Creature from the Black Lagoon' because he bore the brunt of the explosion.

After eating some of the sandwiches we set off in pairs to follow Malc's instructions on how to reach the pit we were to picket. I went with Joe Humphries and despite our slow pace we soon caught up with Keith Smoult. I was as nervous as hell and felt like an escaped POW in wartime Germany. Keith felt the same but Joe was so cool he even went into the local miners' welfare to ask for directions! We tried to act as normally as we could but I felt that everyone could see we were pickets. Keith's nerve broke first when a police car passed and he dashed off into some nearby trees. I was very tempted to follow him but Joe said we were safer on the road, and anyway, we weren't breaking any laws.

After 15 minutes walking we caught our first sight of the pit outlined against the darkening sky. As we approached the pit we stopped dead. The whole of the entrance was crowded with police, the driveway was full of police, and as we got closer we saw the pit canteen was also full of police! It was an unbelievable sight! I've never seen so many police in one place before. My immediate thought was there must be a mass picket in place, or one was expected. We headed for the flat caps visible between the ranks of police. As we arrived we saw there was no mass picket, and a quick chat with one of the half dozen men present told me it was highly unlikely there would be one. The colliery was called Annersley and is in the South Notts Area. I spotted Brian and asked him where the others were and he told me they'd gone down the road to a connected colliery called Newstead. Keith turned up and we chatted with some lads from Grimethorpe who we'd met this morning. There was no sign of humour or piss taking at Annersley. The police seemed to have been hand picked for their height and build, brick shithouses in every sense of the word.

After a few minutes a senior police officer marched across the road and began shouting at us. He said, 'Right, you scum! Stand there, keep still, and don't you dare shout anything at the decent working men coming out! As a matter of fact, don't even breathe too loudly or I'll have you in the back of a van so quickly you won't believe it!!' His tone was very aggressive and I had no doubt he would carry out his threat at the slightest provocation. It was extremely frustrating to have to stand there as the scabs came out and hurled abuse at us!

After a while the rest of the our lads showed up from the other pit but before they could tell us anything about it the senior officer returned and said there were too many of us and if some of us didn't move he would arrest the lot of us for obstruction! What a bloody joke! If anyone was causing an obstruction it was the hundreds of police. There were only about fifteen of us, but to stop the pig carrying out his threat, Keith, Joe, Ian and myself decided to try the pit down the road whilst Brian and Jeff went to get the van so some of the lads could shelter from the rain that had started to come down.

The lane to Newstead ran alongside the colliery buildings and we could see the scabs working beneath the orange lights. We were tempted to shout at them but daren't because the road ahead was pitch black and we didn't know what lay ahead.

We finally arrived at Newstead after getting lost for a while. The colliery lay at the bottom of a road lined with a mixture of condemned and inhabited pit housing. It was a depressing sight and did nothing to calm my jumpy nerves. At the pit there were about half a dozen lads present, including our guide, Malc. They were as cocky as the picket had been at Grimethorpe this morning, taking the piss out of the police. One lad told me this lot were 'green' and were from Devon and Somerset, and as such were easy targets. He also warned us that the next lot, who would be taking over shortly, were real wicked bastards and were from the local police force.

Sure enough, at 9.30pm the 'green' police marched off to be replaced by some of the biggest bastards it has ever been my misfortune to come across. Within minutes four of the Yorkshire lads, including our guide Malc, were unceremoniously thrown into the back of a police van and driven off. I freely admit to being terrified, certain we would be next. Joe wasn't frightened at all and asked a Sergeant if he could give out some leaflets to the scabs who were beginning to arrive. To my great surprise he was allowed to do so, but only on condition that he didn't speak to them, or try to force them to accept a leaflet. Whilst he did this I learned from one of the lads that Malc and his mates had been arrested because they'd been there the night before. I said that wasn't a crime but the lad said being a striking miner, and being there was enough. As we chatted one of the police facing us deliberately stood on my toes, causing me a lot of pain as I tried to get them out from beneath his heavy boots. The bastard had a sadistic grin on his face and only let me go when the others started to move off back up the road. He called me 'Fucking scum' as I limped off, cursing him under my breath. I know who the scum are!

As we walked back to Annersley in the pitch black talking about what we'd seen I almost had a heart attack when two policemen jumped at us, shining torches in our faces and demanding to know where we were going. Joe did the talking until we were asked for our names and addresses. When I told one of them mine he cuffed my ear and warned me not to take the piss! He was finally convinced when I showed him my NUN diary which had my name and address inside. We continued on our way, now completely soaked by the rain which seemed to be getting heavier by the minute.

When we got back to the van we found it full of police taking everyone's details. Joe and Ian managed to squeeze inside but Keith and me were forced to stand outside in the torrential rain. I again had to give my name with the same result minus the cuff round the ear. To my astonishment Keith not only gave a false name and address but he also used the name of one of our Lodge officials as his own! I gasped at his nerve but felt sure he'd be caught out and arrested. Thankfully he wasn't. The police finally left, but warned us that if we were caught in Notts again we would be arrested, and if the van returned it would be impounded! So much for our 'free country'! It is frightening that we, as legitimate trade unionists, should be prevented in such a Draconian way from exercising our democratic right to picket. Welcome to Thatcher's Britain 1984! Orwell wasn't far off the mark!

The journey back to Barnsley was very subdued. Brian was very relieved that he hadn't been arrested as he had been threatened with this morning. We were all totally shocked by our experience, apart from Geordie, and are looking forward to getting home later today. I had to stay up and write all this down whilst it is still fresh in my mind. I'll end with an apt quote from a book I found in this room:

> "A man may perhaps say that the public peace may be hereby disturbed, but he ought to know that there can be no peace where there is no justice, nor any justice if the government instituted for the good of a nation be turned to its ruin."
> Algernon Sidney, 1680.

Thursday March 29th, 1984

We did a final picket at Grimethorpe this morning but all the humour from yesterday had disappeared and we were all feeling a bit downhearted. It was a relief to head back up the M1 and home. On the way we passed a long convoy of lorries heading into Ferrybridge power station which really brought home the full enormity of the task facing us if we are to win this strike. One thing I'm certain about is that the only way we can get the scabs in Notts to join the strike is by mass picketing, and by mass picketing I mean thousands because that's the only way we can beat the police. Those fucking scabs are helping Thatcher to smash the NUM, and if that is allowed to happen it will be a total betrayal of everything our forefathers fought for and the union movement itself will be under threat. Why can't people see that?

Back at Westoe we cleaned out the van before returning it to Newcastle. The GMBU were not pleased to hear their van will be impounded if it's seen in Notts and this may cause us problems if we want to borrow it again.

Back at the picket line the Chairman and Secretary showed their appreciation of our initiative by completely ignoring us, totally disinterested in hearing about the situation in Notts. This sums them up and if we have to rely on useless bastards like them the strike will be lost!

Finally back home I had a much needed bath and then prepared a meal for Kath and the girls in an attempt to soften her up because I left for Notts without seeing her. I just made a quick phonecall that gave her no chance to object. She has forgiven me but I've had to promise her that I'll slow down a bit and take the weekend off so we can spend some time together. Anyway, I'm knackered and could do with a break myself.

Monday April 2nd, 1984

It was nice to have some time off, especially as it gave me the chance to try and explain to Jen and Sasha exactly what's going on. I'm not sure they fully understand but at least they know why I keep disappearing.

I spent the morning going round the shipyards with Peter St Clair, a *Militant* supporter who knows most of the shop stewards. We did quite well, considering three of the yards have been privatised, and the other one had men who seemed to be against unions! We managed to collect £86.25p, and had lots of good arguments with the workers going in. Mind you, I'm getting a bit pissed off with calls for a national ballot. We don't need one because we've voted with our feet, and the majority of miners are out on strike. We need to move forward.

This evening I attended a *Militant* meeting in Newcastle which had Peter Taafe speaking. He's one of their 'leaders' but he doesn't say that. He's not a very good speaker either, seeming more concerned with getting Labour elected than supporting the miners. I hated their way of collecting money. A young lad stood up at the front of the audience and began haranguing them for money to set up a daily paper. He started by asking for someone to donate £100, and when there were no takers, worked his way down to a fiver. I was gobsmacked when a lad stood up and donated his giro cheque! It all seemed stage managed to me and I wasn't impressed.

I was even less impressed afterwards when I spoke to Taafe and he was trying to argue for a national bloody ballot! Very revolutionary. I could've punched the smug git!

Tuesday April 3rd, 1984

I went up to Scotland this afternoon after a quiet morning on the Westoe picket line. The lads just chatted and speculated where the strike is going.

I was invited to go to a miners' benefit for Polmaise Colliery by an old friend of mine, Stuart Hepburn. He's an actor and his theatre company, Badinage, were performing at Fallin Miner's Welfare to raise funds for picketing. Apparently Scotland isn't solid and they're having a lot of problems at Bilston Glen. It was interesting to chat with the pickets and the play itself was very entertaining. Mind you, I did feel a bit guilty coming on my own but Kath was working so I didn't have much choice. At least it made for a nice change.

SOCIALISM & CASH

Monday April 9th, 1984
This morning I was given a letter of authorisation from the Lodge which allows me to collect funds on their behalf. Apathy and lack of action has seen us end the unofficial strike committee and I handed over all monies we had to the Treasurer. Nowt happened last week except daily visits to the Westoe picket, and nowt happened there either.

This afternoon I went on a tour of various workplaces in Newcastle with Geoff Price of *Militant*. He is also on the Regional Executive of the Labour Party and so carries more clout than myself, a mere miner. We visited the Fire Brigades Union in Newcastle and received a good reception. Their Secretary told us that he wasn't surprised at the Notts miners because during their national strike the Notts firemen were very reluctant to take part and support everyone else. He also joked that the Notts men were carried around in buckets because they have no backbone. He has promised to support us in any way he can, including asking his members to join our picket lines. Very encouraging.

Later we paid a visit to 'The Duck' which is Wearmouth's strike centre. I was very impressed with their set up, which includes maps on the wall with every open cast site in the North East marked on it. Stan Pearce, their Lodge Delegate, gave me a letter which appeals to trade unionists for support and funds. I intend asking our Lodge Secretary if we can get something similar done for when we collect funds because it's better than the letter I got this morning.

Tuesday April 10th, 1984
15 men were arrested this morning at the Deerness open cast site near Tow Law in Durham, including Bob Clay, the Labour MP for Sunderland North. I was told that he was arrested when trying to rescue a picket being savagely kicked by the riot police, or SPG as they are known. Hundreds of pickets marched to

the police station where they were being held to protest. Mass pickets are now to be held there every day in an attempt to stop the scab lorries from moving coal because every nut of coal moved is a threat to the strike. I want to go but have been told that because I'm a good talker my fund raising is just as important. I'm not convinced but will continue for the time being.

Wednesday April 11th, 1984

This evening I went to an SWP meeting in Newcastle. The speaker was a man called John Deason and the subject was 'The Miners Strike and the Struggle for Socialism'. It was an excellent meeting with lots of debate and questions. I agreed with everything I heard. Also present were Joe Humphries, Ian Wilburn, Keith Smoult and Dave Farham, with Ian and Joe joining the party. I'm still not sure but what I do know is that what they are saying is a lot more constructive than what *Militant* are saying. I was given £120 and it was suggested that we keep it in reserve in case we ever need money the Lodge won't supply. I'm regretting now handing over the reserves we had but there's nothing can be done about that now. I bumped into Geoff Price as I was going to the meeting and felt guilty because I didn't tell him where I was going. Kath made me feel even more guilty when I got home, complaining that she seldom sees me these days, and neither do the girls.

Thursday April 12th, 1984

I have spent a wasted day going around Newcastle with Geoff Price, though it's not his fault. It has been spending the day with him that has finally made me decide to join the SWP. He has obviously been aware of my interest in the SWP and has tried everything he knows to turn me against them. He calls them a bunch of middle class students who are only committed until they graduate; then they will suddenly become middle class again. In my opinion this is a very insulting and narrow minded point of view. There are thousands of working class kids who are in colleges and universities who are well aware of the evils of capitalism and want to change it. *Militant* are hot air and don't appear to understand the slogan 'Unity is strength'. Neither do NACODS who yesterday voted narrowly to join the strike, but not by the two thirds majority required, so they stay at work. If they came out the strike would be won. Why can't they see that?

Friday April 13th, 1984

I met up with Yunus, an SWP member, in Newcastle this morning. He is a really committed activist who I've seen a lot of over the past few weeks. He does have one fault, he's a Hull City fan, but I suppose someone has to be! Anyway, I finally did it and joined the SWP, though not sure Friday 13th was the right day to do it!

The SWP have invited my family and myself down to the Derbyshire Miners Holiday Camp in Skegness for the Easter weekend. Kath is not very keen because she says it will be too political and she has no interest in politics, but the fact that she supports me and hates Thatcher makes her political whether she likes it or not. Anyway, I've managed to persuade her that it will be a nice break and there will be plenty to keep her and the girls occupied away from politics and no one will put any pressure on her. The fact that it is a free holiday means we won't be out of pocket because the SWP is paying. She is only getting £47 a week from her job, and though we are better off than a lot of miners, it aint a fortune so I refuse to feel guilty. I'm sick of feeling guilty.

Monday April 16th, 1984

I visited Parsons this morning with Bob Murdoch, an SWP member who works there. He introduced me to a shop steward who told us that the Secretary wasn't there but to come back on Wednesday to do a bucket collection, and also to bring some literature which they could put up on the union notice board to explain what the strike was about.

Bob gave me £25 from his union to spend on picketing so the trip wasn't entirely wasted. Travel expenses are a bit of a burden so I asked the Lodge to help and they agreed to give me £1 which will help. I was getting lifts off John McIvor but strangely his car was written off when it was parked outside of a bank and was smashed into by a car driven by a policeman! Coincidence?

Tuesday April 17th, 1984

I almost got arrested in Eldon Square shopping centre, Newcastle, this morning. I was doing a bucket collection outside Virgin Records when I had a heated argument with a bunch of Tory students I had previously encountered at Newcastle Poly. Minutes after they left a policeman turned up and threatened to arrest me if I didn't move on immediately. He wasn't nasty about it and said he was from a mining family himself and had a brother on strike but the law is the law and must be enforced. I didn't argue too much and left but I really can't see what crime I was supposed to be committing.

Wednesday April 18th, 1984

Keith Smoult and myself returned to Parsons this morning and ended up having a blazing row with a union official. We had returned as requested and reported to the union office. An official there told us to come back next week because today was the centenary of the company being formed and the site was crawling with dignitaries. We had a bit of fraternal argument with the man and told him we had no intention of standing on company property but he was insistent so we reluctantly agreed to leave though we were mad as hell at the wasted journey and expense. We left him with some leaflets and a letter appealing for funds.

As Keith and I headed to the nearest Metro station we met two lads from the SWP, complete with buckets and papers to sell. They were equally angry when we told them what happened because they'd made a special effort to come along. After a short discussion we decided to start a bucket collection outside of the gates.

We were doing well until a suit and tie official turned up and started calling us liars and communists, accusing us of not being miners at all but collecting for the SWP. He really wound me up and I angrily showed him my letter of authorisation and tried to explain why we had started collecting. He yelled at me and threatened to get the police so we decided to cut our losses and leave. We had collected £14.65 and yet another example of how some union officials are rubbish and care more about the bosses than their members!

Friday April 20th, 1984

Well, here we are in Skegness, nicely settled in. We have been given a lovely bungalow and the girls are in a nearby children's dormitory.

The journey down was a bit uncomfortable because the minibus was a bit overcrowded but our driver, Anne, was excellent, and the journey only took 5 hours so it wasn't too bad.

After registering we explored the camp, and to my relief we discovered there is plenty to keep Kath and the girls occupied. Jennifer and Sasha are thoroughly enjoying themselves and have already made loads of friends. I doubt they will sleep much because the dormitory was full of noisy kids when I looked in at 10.30. As long as they are happy is all that matters, and it will allow Kath and myself to spend some time together and that is very important just now because the strike is beginning to cause us problems. Hopefully we can sort it out.

I was pleased to discover that Jim Tierney is here because I met him up in Scotland the other week and we have a mutual friend in Stuart Hepburn. Also, the programme for the weekend looks very interesting, with Paul Foot of the *Daily Mirror* being the speaker I am most looking forward to seeing.

Sunday April 22nd, 1984

I've just had a great night out with Dave and Jean, Anne and Paul. It was just nice to relax and chat with friends. We also had a useful chat with Ian Mitchell's wife, Mandy, who gave us a lot of advice on fundraising, and also urged us to set up a Women's Support Group so that wives and girlfriends can get actively involved in the strike, because it affects their future just as much as the men. Kath agrees that it's a good idea but says her job at the Women's Refuge means she won't be able to get involved.

Paul Foot was excellent this morning in his talk about George Orwell. He said that *Homage to Catalonia* is by far Orwell's best book and I look forward to reading it when this is all over. Strangely enough Kath enjoyed the talk as well. I say strange because she openly admits to having never enjoyed reading a book. Whatever, I'm glad she enjoyed something political.

Yesterday was a good day as well but I got so pissed I couldn't stand, let alone write! One thing did mar an otherwise great day and that was the appearance of a scab from Ollerton Colliery in Notts. The cheeky bastard turned up with three of his mates who claimed to be striking miners. I didn't believe them because no striker worth his salt would ever be seen associating with a scab. I had been sitting in the Drifter bar having a good time when Yunus came over and said there were some striking miners from Notts outside who wanted to talk to some miners. Dave Farham and me went outside to meet them on the balcony but they were already talking to some Yorkshire pickets so we just listened. We were amazed to hear one of them actually admitting to being a 'working miner', and not only that, the bastard was proud of himself! My first reaction was to throw him off the balcony but a lad called Steve Hammill, who I recognised as the miner who spoke at the Tony Cliff meeting in Sheffield, talked me out of it and started to argue the case why all miners should be supporting the strike. I went to the bog to calm down but when I came back I saw Ian Mitchell had to hold Steve back! The scab took the hint and left but he spoilt our night because from then on scabs were the main topic of our conversation.

Monday April 23rd, 1984

Tony Cliff gave an excellent summing up of the strike so far and urged us all to go back and argue the case for making the strike solid by mass picketing and to appeal to rank and file trade unionists to get their unions to support us. We ended by singing the *Internationale* but I hate communal singing and felt embarrassed, though I did like the words.

The girls couldn't stop talking about the great time they had and the friends they'd made. They were sad to leave, and so were Kath and me. We agreed it was the best holiday we'd ever had, and I feel ready to continue the strike reinvigorated.

Tuesday April 24th, 1984

I dragged myself out of my nice warm bed at 4.30am to go picketing at

Tow Law. I'm fed up with just collecting and want to be more active, and besides, more men have been arrested since Bob Clay.

It was bloody freezing out there and the only way for us to keep warm was by burning some old tractor tires one of the lads found. They kept us warm but the muck blowing about made us all look like we'd done a shift down the pit.

There were about 200 men present but we didn't manage to stop a single lorry going in or out. No union officials were there and the police present had no problems at all. It was obvious to me that we had to block the road somehow but no one was interested in listening to me when I suggested putting the burning tires in the road. If we are not careful men will stop coming because of inactivity.

When we got back to the pit I asked the Lodge Treasurer if we could have some funds to buy hot food for the pickets at Tow Law, as other lodges were doing for their pickets. He claimed that our funds are 'tied up'. I argued that we have about 70 men going each day, and that the Lodge can afford to give each car a £5 fuel allowance for the 70 mile round trip so why not about £20 to get hot food and drink to the lads? Same reply about funds being 'tied up'. Bloody pathetic!

So, Ian Wilburn and myself have decided to use the £150 already collected to get pies each day, and we can continue to raise funds to keep it going. Hopefully we will shame the lodge officials to take over once we have started. We met a baker on Boldon lane and he has agreed to bake us 70 pies a day to start off with, and Ian and myself will take them up to the picket line each day.

Wednesday April 25th, 1984
Our first lot of pies cost £13 and we delivered them to the lads using 'Tonto' Jackson's car. The lads really appreciated it, though they still didn't do anything more than shout a bit when the scab lorries went in and out.

A meeting was held in the Armstrong Hall to discuss the idea of forming a Women's Support Group, and to my great surprise about 200 women turned up. The meeting was organised by Margaret Reavey, a *Militant* supporter, and one of the few who have spoken to me since I joined the SWP. She had invited me to speak about fundraising, which I did.

The outcome of this first meeting is the formation of the Westoe Miners Wives Support Group, with Anne Kendrick elected as Secretary, and Ann Hall as Treasurer. Unfortunately their first task is to find somewhere to work from because the Lodge officials have refused to let them use the Armstrong Hall, because 'it would be too noisy with a load of kids running around'. Honestly, they are a fucking joke and totally out of touch with reality!! Thank god we don't have to rely on them to win this strike!

Friday April 27th, 1984

We did the pie run to Tow Law this morning but the whole thing is a bit dispiriting because of the passivity of the pickets.

This evening I was invited by the Gateshead Trades Council to attend a May Day event at the Guildhall in Newcastle. It's now 2.30am and I have just finished counting the collection that was taken. There is £156 altogether, including a cheque for £50 from a man who would only say his family had all been miners and that he could easily afford it. I asked him to make the cheque out to the Lodge, not wanting it to be made out to myself for obvious reasons. The rest of the money will go into the 'pie fund', which is exactly what I appealed for when I was allowed to make a short speech in the interval. The audience were great and it gave me a personal boost to speak again in public. I had a great night, getting on particularly well with an SWP member called Mick Armstrong. He drove me home through fog so thick you could cut it with a knife. I hope he got back home alright.

Saturday April 28th, 1984

For some strange reason today was designated May Day in Newcastle and a march and rally had been organised to mark the event. The SWP were out in force to sell *Socialist Worker*, as well as distributing hundreds of 'Victory to the Miners' placards, especially to miners who were present, though a lot of them ripped the Socialist Workers Party logo from the top which I found petty and downright ungrateful. I had brought along a plastic bucket covered in 'Coal Not Dole' stickers to collect for the Women's Support Group. Ian Wilburn had brought a van full of women up to collect as well.

As we stood chatting we were approached by a Northumberland NUM official who asked me what I intended doing with the bucket. His tone gave me a few ideas but I contented myself with telling him the truth. To my amazement he said I was not allowed to collect on behalf of the miners, and it was his opinion that the money wouldn't even go to the miners. Here we go again, I thought. I told him I was a striking miner and he demanded to know where I was from. I could have shown him the Lodge letter but his belligerent tone really got my back up so I told him it was none of his business, and anyway, how did I know HE was a miner. This plainly shocked him because like a lot of union officials they have an inflated sense of their own importance. He told me who he was in an offended tone whilst a group of tough looking Northumberland miners gathered around him and a very angry exchange of words took place, culminating in him threatening to have me arrested if I made any attempt to collect. That did shock me and I asked him why he was so against me collecting. He replied, 'The Northumberland miners do not go begging or accept charity.' I pointed out that I was not one of his men and that it was not begging but asking fellow workers to help us in our fight. I added that he had better get used to it because it could be a long strike and we would need all the help we could get if we were to beat Thatcher and her boot boys. He just repeated his threat and said he had been fighting for his members since before I was born and there was nothing I could tell him about strikes. With that him and his henchmen stormed off to take their places at the front of the march. Anne Kendrick said he might be able to have me arrested but he wouldn't dare do it to them so they decided to do the collecting.

We marched proudly through the streets of Newcastle, cheered on by the shoppers. The rally was in Leazes Park and we arrived there in brilliant sunshine and found a place to sit to listen to the speeches and to count the money the lasses had collected.

The speeches were full of the usual rhetoric from a poor selection of speakers, and it was only when Denis Murphy, President of the Northumberland miners, got up to speak did I pay any attention. First of all he claimed that Thomas Hepburn was a Northumberland miner when in fact he was a Durham miner and founded one of the first ever unions in 1832. Then he boasted that his men were the best in the coalfields and had been solidly behind the strike since day one. Wrong again because we had to picket the buggers out at Ellington. I don't mean to sound petty but facts are facts.

The biggest shock came when Tom Sawyer of NUPE came onto the platform and presented Murphy with a cheque for £20,000! For a union who 'doesn't accept charity' this struck me as the height of hypocrisy and I couldn't restrain myself any longer. I rushed to the front of the platform and shouted, 'I thought the Northumberland miners didn't accept charity'? Anne Kendrick joined me and also attacked him, much to the concern of some officials who came running over to us and begged us to desist in the name of solidarity. We shut up and returned to our group because we'd made our point. However I was still furious at the hypocrisy of that bloody official threatening to have me arrested for collecting coins whilst they eagerly accepted a cheque for 20 grand!! Bastards!

As the speeches ended we began to leave but a furious woman started shouting at me, accusing me of trying to use the women for my own political ends. When I learned she was Mrs Geoff Price the attack made more sense but was still laughable. *Militant* indeed.

Before I left the park I saw a stand run by the Newcastle Gay and

Lesbian group that made tin badges to order with a little machine they had. They offered to make me badges for a cut price 10p each if I would sign a petition supporting them. I would have signed it anyway but had 20 badges made that said 'Westoe Miners – Zulu Pickets'. I intend selling them for 20p each, all profit into the 'pie fund'. They told me they'll make more at the same price but I'll see how these go first.

I made my way down to Jarrow where Neil Kinnock was unveiling a plaque on the Metro station to commemorate the famous Jarrow Marchers. When I arrived I met up with comrades from the SWP and we watched Kinnock pose for pictures with three old men who were amongst the last survivors of the march before making a short speech and unveiling the plaque. He then set off with his entourage to march through the streets of Jarrow to a community centre where he was due to speak. We were disgusted to see that one of the old men was left standing on the platform alone with no one taking any notice of him, poor sod, so a couple of lads went to get him a taxi whilst we ran to catch up with the march. The old man had served his purpose and then been abandoned. So much for socialism, eh?

We caught up and positioned ourselves right behind Kinnock and the other so called dignitaries, proudly carrying our 'Victory to the Miners' placards. I have quite a loud voice, some would call it a big mouth, and I used it to great effect, shouting at Kinnock to get off the fence and support the miners, repeating it until he reached the sanctuary of the community centre. Our Lodge banner and officials were directly behind and the looks on their faces told me exactly what they felt about my performance. Still, I expect they got their chance to suck up to Kinnock inside, and I went home to sleep soundly in my bed.

Monday April 30th, 1984

Went picketing at Tow Law and again there were about 200 men present. Unfortunately a lot of them seemed content to warm their arses against the blazing tyres. Even when we had a push against the police to try and close the gates to the site most of the buggers just stood and watched. Why do they come if they don't want to fight? A policeman had his arm broken in the push but it was the scab lorry speeding through the gate to blame, not us.

That was the only bit of excitement in a dull morning, apart from the arrival of Ian and Tonto with the pies, which caused a stampede. I sold all 20 badges and got orders for dozens more. At this rate we'll be able to finance the pies just from the sale of badges!

ZULU, ZULU, ZULU

Tuesday May 1st, 1984
This morning at Tow Law one of the younger lads, Mickey Hoy, stood solid as a rock for three hours holding a 'Stop the Police State' placard, face to face with a policeman. He was only prevented from continuing by the appearance of the lorries giving the pig an excuse to punch Mickey in the face. This cowardly act was seen by lots of pickets who responded by surging forward in an attempt to get revenge. Yet a-bloody-gain it was the passivity of our own men that prevented us gaining the upper hand. The idle bastards just stood by and watched, even when a few of the lads were snatched from the front row and arrested. They just watched as we tried to rescue them but were defeated by lack of numbers. We have to overcome this passivity if we are to have any chance of achieving anything here. Once again the most positive response of the morning was the arrival of the pies. I hoped some of the bastards would choke on them so we could stand and watch!

Wednesday May 2nd, 1984
This morning I suggested that we try the 'Gandhi' tactic of passive resistance and I sat myself down in the middle of the road, urging others to follow. Predictably only 20 or so lads followed whilst the majority stood by and laughed, treating it all as a huge bloody joke. The bastards watched as the police casually dragged us off the road and threw us into the mud at the roadside. One Westoe lad, Manny Benham, was thrown straight into the back of a police van as had been promised by an Inspector yesterday when Manny had the audacity to answer him back. That's British justice for you! At least the lad had the guts to try and do something positive. It is all getting very frustrating.

Thursday May 3rd, 1984
Tonto Jackson was arrested this morning for having the misfortune to be

standing too close to a lorry which had its windscreen smashed. The pigs just grabbed him as the nearest person to the crime. He has been charged with using 'foul and abusive language' because he swore when the pigs roughly grabbed him.

After Tonto's arrest we tried a new tactic, walking in front of the scab lorries at a snail's pace, linking arms so the pigs couldn't arrest us easily. It worked brilliantly but despite us shouting for more men, not enough of us were prepared to take part. The pigs charged into us and tried to break our ranks, and even though we put up a brave struggle we couldn't stop them from achieving their aim. I was linked in with Arthur Oxley from Vane Tempest Colliery. I know Arthur from Broad Left meetings and you couldn't pick a better man to be standing next to in a fight because he's well over six foot with a build to match. He was my saviour this morning because he refused to let go of me as I was dragged to the side of the road. The look on the young pig's face when he realised he was on his own was a real picture. Arthur said, 'What are you going to do now, son, because you can't arrest us both?' He took the wise decision to let me go and beat a hasty retreat. The battle was over but the war isn't won and I'm pretty sure the two of us will have to be on our guard from now on.

The pigs made ten arrests this morning and the mood of the men seems to be getting more militant, thank god. The Westoe men are getting really wound up by the lads we have had arrested.

The pies arrived a bit late because of Tonto's arrest. His bail conditions state he's not allowed within 2 miles of Tow Law so one of the lads dropped him off and delivered the pies and then picked him up on the way back. The arrest of the 'pie man' has done the trick in terms of ending Westoe passivity. You have to laugh.

Kath is very worried I am going to be arrested after I told her about this morning's events. I've told her not to worry because even if I am arrested I'll only get fined. She remains unconvinced that what we are doing is lawful and this has caused even more friction between us. I feel she is allowing herself to be influenced by the media who seem to be engaged in a daily propaganda campaign against the NUM, and Arthur Scargill in particular. I feel she is coming round to our side but at the moment she still needs to be convinced we can win. We can if we can convince the rest of the trade union movement of the justice of our fight. If only they would black coal and refuse to use imported oil. If only the scabs would see sense and that their jobs are at risk as well. If only NACODS would join us we would be guaranteed victory. It's been 8 weeks and no sign of an end in sight so Tony Cliff has been proved right so far. This isn't '72 and '74, more's the pity.

Anyway, attitudes on the picket line seem to be hardening and Westoe has gained quite a few new pickets.

Friday May 4th, 1984

This morning's picket at Tow Law was quiet until 10am when 3 lorries approached the entrance. We tried the same tactic as yesterday and poured onto the road linking arms in front of the first lorry. Yet again there must have been over 200 men present but only about 70 of us were prepared to get involved whilst the idle bastards just watched. It was those bastards who were responsible for 17 of us getting lifted this morning, not the pigs! Our union officials should be there giving a lead and taking the names of those people not involved and stopping their £2 picket money. If the buggers weren't getting paid they wouldn't turn up! Bastards!!

As we moved onto the road we took the police by surprise. I was right in front of the leading lorry, swearing up at the scab driver for helping the Tories. It didn't take the pigs long to organise themselves and storm into action and I quickly found myself grabbed round the throat from behind. Unlike yesterday there was no big Arthur to rescue me and despite my vainly trying to put up a struggle I quickly found myself being forcibly dragged by two pigs into the site where open police vans were waiting for us. I was thrown violently against the side of a van and a pig kicked my ankles and told me to spread my legs, just like they do on TV cop shows when they search people for weapons. This bastard added a knee in the small of my back as he roughly searched me. There was no bloody need for his violence as I'd done nothing to resist, but that didn't stop him from pushing me hard into the back of a van. As I went in I heard Arthur's voice saying, 'There's no fucking need to be so tough, ya bastard.' When he saw me he added, 'I thought we were going to see the week out, young un.' Before I could reply I landed on the floor of the van, hurting my arm as I fell. I pulled myself up and sat on the benches which ran either side of the van. Within minutes I was joined by Ian Wilburn who sat next to me and pretty soon the van was full with six pigs and six pickets. Ian remarked how strange it was that within days the men who delivered the pies, and the one who raised the money were all arrested. I said I hoped the bastards who had stood watching us starved to death.

Just before we reached our destination the bench Ian, Mick, me and three pigs were sitting on collapsed beneath us and made us burst out laughing. The pigs weren't amused and accused us of breaking it deliberately. I blamed all those pies which made us laugh even harder. We were almost hysterical when we found out we were in Crook police station. It just struck us as really funny. Crook!

We were taken out of the van one at a time and made to queue outside until our turn came. Inside we were ordered to remove our belts and take everything from our pockets. I was asked my name and yet again was told not to try and be fucking funny. They must have checked me out somehow because then they started to take the piss with jokes I'd heard a hundred times before, simple bastards! After answering their routine questions I was photographed with the two arresting officers either side of me. They spoiled a lovely picture! They used a Polaroid camera and assured us the photographs would be destroyed at a later date, lying bastards! I was then led to a cell and told to remove my boots. The smell from my socks even made me feel sick!

I was soon joined by two Westoe lads, Martin Quantrill and Mick Myers. They complained about my smelly feet but their farting did nothing to enhance the Spartan cell, or should that be Spartan smell? We discussed how we were arrested before Mick and me were taken out to meet Tommy Callan, Durham Area General Secretary, who took our names so he could get us legal representation. He also offered to inform our families but I refused because I didn't want to worry Kath while she was at work, confident I would soon be out. Tommy gave us each a cigarette to take back to our cells. We were told we had been charged with Obstruction of the Highway and Tommy told us we would be appearing in Bishop Auckland Magistrates court at 2pm.

At 1pm we were taken in a police car to Bishop Auckland and put in a cell beneath the court. The three of us were absolutely starving, not having eaten since early morning so we were overjoyed when a hatch in the door opened and a pig asked if we wanted pineapple on our gammon steak? I told him I was a vegetarian but he said it was OK, I could just have the pineapple. This made the lads howl with laughter but I wasn't amused! The lads were surprised that the food on offer seemed so good, but they were even more surprised 20 minutes later when the hatch opened and a plate of stale meat paste sandwiches were passed through by a broadly grinning pig. All of us burst out laughing, seeing the funny side of our own naivety and rolling about the cell floor laughing like loonies. At least we'd retained our sense of humour.

My court appearance didn't take long. The female magistrate tried to suppress a grin as my name was read out. Then remanded me on bail with the condition that I not go within 2 miles of Tow Law until my court appearance. Martin and Mick got the same. Then we were given back our meagre possessions and released.

Nine Westoe lads had been arrested so Durham sent the Executive coach to take us back to South Shields. Back at Westoe we were warned by our own officials not to break the bail conditions and then left to make our own way home. Those bastards didn't give a shit about any of us and they did nothing for the morale of men who had sacrificed for the union. I really do hate them!

Kath was upset when I told her what happened but again I had to remind her that I had been shouting my mouth off since Scargill was elected and couldn't stay in the background. I hope she understands but I'm not sure she really does.

FLYING SQUAD

Monday May 7th, 1984
Since I, and quite a few others are now banned from picketing at Tow Law, we were asked if we wanted to go away on flying picket duty. I got a phone call this morning from the Lodge Secretary asking if I could go. I said yes straightaway, grateful for the chance to stay active. We are heading for Lancashire where there are still pits working. As soon as I put the phone down I picked it up again and rang Kath to break the news. She took the news surprisingly well and wished me good luck. I told her we should be back before the weekend. I felt a lot easier in my mind with her backing. We had to be at the Armstrong Hall for 3pm.

After packing my holdall I received a call from Mike Simons of the SWP asking for news. When I told him we were heading for Lancs he gave me the phone numbers of comrades in Manchester who I can call if we need accommodation. We both agreed that our most likely target is Agecroft Colliery because that's where the local union officials have told their members to ignore picket lines. Bloody disgusting! I promised to keep Mike informed of any newsworthy events because he is one of the people who write *Socialist Worker*.

At the Armstrong Hall the 15 of us going were given £32 subsistence allowance from the Durham NUM which is to make sure we can eat. The Secretary told us all to be careful and not to forget to keep in touch with our families because he didn't want worried wives ringing him to find out what was happening.

There were about 60 pickets at the hall and there was a lot of bad feeling about only 15 of us being allowed to go, with the majority view being that as many men wanting to go should be allowed to go. I agreed, but the Secretary explained that he had no say in the matter and the decision had been made by the Area Executive. He added that all the Lodges have been split into four groups, with each group consisting of four pits who would work together as picketing teams. Westoe has been teamed with

Sacriston, Wearmouth, and Herrington, and these pits will work together on all future flying pickets.

The coach finally arrived with 10 pickets from Sacriston on board and we loaded our bags into the boot. The coach then headed to Wearmouth where we picked up 20 men, then finally down to Herrington where the final 10 boarded. Fully loaded we set off for Lancashire with only the few officials on board knowing exactly where we were going, and they refused to tell us, though god knows why. It's not as if we could tell anyone.

The journey took about three hours and I passed the time chatting with the lad next to me, Gary Marshall, to whom I'd sold a few copies of *Socialist Worker*. We got on really well and have a lot in common. He told me he is growing increasingly disillusioned with the Labour Party and has been a member for 13 years. He hates Kinnock, more now because of his almost total lack of support for us miners, and he said he agrees with a lot of stuff he reads in the paper. I think he's got real potential to join the Party so we agreed to try and stick together on this picket.

We arrived at Bold Miners Welfare to find it full to capacity with Durham miners. I recognised loads of faces and was pleased to see big Arthur, who bought me a pint, but before we could settle in the order came to get back onto the coach because we were heading to Manchester where accommodation had been arranged for us in a social club in Eccles.

We arrived at the Greenbank Labour Club around 9pm and a lot of the lads were whingeing about not being able to stay in Bold. I discovered that quite a few of them had been in Bold last week and had managed to fix themselves up with comfortable lodgings and they were pissed off because they were too far away to take advantage. The club was full of people celebrating the Bank Holiday and watching the Davis – White snooker final on a big TV screen. We struggled through the crowd with our luggage and sleeping bags and followed a woman upstairs where she showed us the room we would be sleeping in. She welcomed us and said we could stay for the week and that alternative accommodation would be fixed in people's homes in the morning though probably not for all of us. I told Gary I was going to phone some contacts in Manchester to try and get us somewhere to stay.

I phoned a woman called Irene Davis and she told me to ring a guy called Phil Ramsall, which I did. He has given me the address of a guy called Mick Brightman who only lives five minutes away. Phil told me to ring him again in the morning after picket duty. I told our union man where we were going and he wasn't too pleased and said we should all stick together. We still insisted on going and he told us to be back at the club for 4.15am!

After a few wrong turnings and some directions from a pub we found the house we were looking for. We were nervous about knocking on a stranger's door but it was bloody freezing so I knocked gingerly. The door was opened by a smiling face who welcomed us into a lovely warm room whilst he went off to the kitchen. He returned minutes later with coffee and egg sandwiches, and while we ate he asked a stream of questions about the strike in Durham. He told us that him and his wife Jane were students but that he had been involved in a strike at a place called Gardners that had lasted 26 weeks!! We said ours wouldn't last that long but that we couldn't imagine how hard it must have been for him. He introduced us to Jane and she told us they were both studying hard for exams. We took the hint and said we'd like to sleep if it was possible because we had to be back at the club for 4am. He told us to make ourselves at home. He showed us into his front room which was full of books and had a bed settee. I was amazed at the books, being an avid reader myself, but Gary reminded me we needed to sleep so we settled down, top to toe on the settee, and within minutes Gary was knocking out zeds like a pig.

Tuesday May 8th, 1984

Gary said he had a job waking me up and we left the house as quietly as we could so we didn't wake our hosts, not even to make a cup of coffee. I was still half asleep but the cold air outside soon woke me up and we walked briskly back to the club without getting lost.

The scene at the club made us realise how fortunate we'd been. There were men lying asleep on every available seat, the floor was covered in fag ends and the few tables were full of empty beer glasses. Two lads were playing pool, the pockets stuffed with paper to save money, and another lad was making tea in a small kitchen. He told us they'd been drinking until well after two and the lads awake hadn't slept at all. Our union official came bursting into the room wearing a cowboy hat and firing a plastic gun which he used to wake the sleeping men! They told him where to stick his stupid gun but woke up anyway. He ordered us all outside and we shivered as we waited. The coach driver finally showed up at 5.15 and swore that was the time he'd been told to arrive. Our union man was given loads of abuse for robbing us of valuable sleeping time but he kept insisting it was the driver's fault. I believed the driver.

The coach smelled foul with stale beer and farts and I was relieved when we arrived at Agecroft. Fresh air never smelled so good! We had to walk a few hundred yards to the colliery and were surprised to pass a power station next to the pit, which was bloody handy for them. As we got close to the pit entrance we began to run, chanting 'Zulu' in the hope it would scare the pigs. It didn't. We were expecting to join a mass picket but instead there were no more than a hundred of us present, and twice as many police lining the road. We joined the picket and I asked a lad where the hell everyone else was. He said they'd gone to a pit called Parkside which was also scabbing. One of our lads, Peter Farrish, provided us with some humour by walking up and down the police lines squeaking a toy pig he'd brought along, much to the annoyance of the real pigs. I couldn't see him getting away with it for much longer, and sure enough when a push began at the arrival of the first scabs the pigs jumped on him and he was hauled away, as was another lad. All we'd achieved was two arrests but at least the push had warmed us up, and everyone got stuck in, which made a nice change.

As soon as we'd lost one nutter, another made his presence known. He is a local striker called Stan and he made Peter seem like an intellectual! He had odd socks, one yellow the other green, into which his trousers were tucked, and he had a weird woolly hat sticking up on his head. He blew on a mouth organ and shouted obscure statements such as, 'Agecroft, you are doomed', and, 'Who invented steam engine Agecroft?' At least he added a bit of colour and humour to an otherwise depressing morning as the scabs streamed into the pit, not even stopping to talk to the six pickets the pigs had allowed to stand at the gate. Some of the scabs were being taken into the pit by what looked like public transport buses, and if they were public transport it was outrageous because the drivers had to be in the TGWU who had been asked not to cross our lines. I told our union official to investigate when we got back into Manchester. Stan, in one of his more lucid moments, pointed to some men we could see at a window across the road drying dishes and told us they were the Agecroft union officials and that the canteen was full of pigs kept in reserve in case of trouble. If what Stan says is true then it really really pisses me off and is the worst example of back stabbing from NUM officials I have ever seen! Those bastards are feeding the thugs who beat us!

At 9.30 our coach returned and took us to Manchester Poly where we were provided with breakfast of rolls and coffee. We really appreciated the solidarity they were showing us. I got a shock when I heard my name being announced over the tannoy system asking me to go to the nearest phone. I thought something had happened at home as I anxiously picked up the phone. I was genuinely relieved to find it was only Phil Ramsall wanting to talk. He came up to the dining area and I introduced him to Gary. We talked about the morning picket, then he asked if we would be prepared to speak at some meetings and visit some workplaces. We agreed provided he can get us transport. I also said we felt that Mick's family could do without us as they prepare for exams and a quick call fixed us up with a new place to stay. He drove us to Salford and chatted all the way about what he hoped we could achieve during our stay. He is very enthusiastic and I like that.

In Salford he introduced us to Hilary Burke who has a spare room in her house. She also made us feel at home, making coffee and asking us lots of questions about how the strike is going in Durham. She'd put some lads from Easington the previous week and they'd told her the strike was unlikely to last in Durham area because the majority of men are moderate. I told her about the passivity of our pickets but also said I thought the strike would stay solid now we were out.

She took us to a small factory where we did a paper sale and did a bucket collection. Gary really seemed to enjoy the paper sale and grew in confidence as we stood there. We only sold a few papers and collected a few quid but at least we felt we were doing something useful. Hilary then drove us back to the club so we could tell our union man where we were going. She also said she could find accommodation for another two men and would prefer it if they were a bit political. I think she means potential SWP members. We had already met two lads from Wearmouth, John and Keith, so we found them and asked them if they'd like alternative digs. They were delighted after having spent a really uncomfortable night in the club and jumped at the chance. They went to tell their union man and we agreed to meet them after we'd collected our stuff from Mick's place. Again our man was stroppy about it and accused us of being snobby, daft bastard. I asked if the coach could pick us up in Salford and he said no. I asked if we were going to be at Agecroft all week and he said he didn't know. I couldn't be arsed to argue with him so I gave him Hilary's phone number in case he needed to reach us and said we'd make our own way to Agecroft. Gary and me went round to Mick's and explained why we were moving. Mick was great and said if he could last 26 weeks then so could we. We said we hoped we'd win long before that, and after a brief meeting with his daughter, who had never met a miner before and was disappointed we had to leave, we walked back to the club with our gear.

As we waited outside for Hilary some of our lads confronted us and again we were accused of being 'snobby bastards'. They asked why we hadn't invited Westoe lads to come with us. I told them the truth and tried to explain about the SWP but they were unconvinced and told us to fuck off. Fair enough. I did feel a bit guilty though.

Hilary picked us all up and drove us back to her place. She introduced us to a friend of hers called Bobby who was visiting from Southampton and has been in the SWP for a long time. We decided to go out for a walk to explore the area and also decided to eat out to save Hilary the trouble so we all had a Chinese takeaway.

We got back to Hilary's to discover she had made a huge pan of curry! None of us mentioned our meal and we all had a huge plate, laughing like loonies when the lasses left the room. No chance of us starving just yet!

Gary and the lads went out for a pint but I decided to stay behind so I could write. Of course they thought I was interested in the two lasses judging by the nudges and winks but they couldn't have been more wrong. Hilary was busy so I chatted with Bobby who was enthusiastic about an author called Victor Serge. I intend reading him soon as I get the chance.

John and Keith have been given a room up the road with a woman called Anne Robertson, and Gary and I are in a spare room. He claimed the only mattress, giving a bad back as an excuse, and I'm in a sleeping bag on the floor. We can have a lie in tomorrow because Hilary has some meetings planned in Manchester so we'll miss the picket. Two less won't make a difference. 200 extra just might!

Wednesday May 9th, 1984

What a stinking bastard day! No, that's not quite accurate because the day was OK. It's the evening that was a bastard but I'll get to that later!

We had a nice lie in and breakfast before heading for Manchester Free Trade Hall where teachers were to discuss their pay claim. They were meeting to talk about what action to take in support of their pay claim which the Tory government had rejected. I stood outside selling *Socialist Worker* with a woman called Irene Davis as the delegates went in. She told me we were standing on the site of the Peterloo massacre and though the name sounded familiar I didn't know what that was. She enlightened me by explaining that thousands of workers had attended a meeting there in 1819 and the troops had slaughtered dozens of innocent people with no provocation. Irene asked me if I would be prepared to address the meeting being held inside though the delegates would have to vote on the motion first. I agreed though felt very nervous about the prospect of actually speaking.

I was taken into the meeting by Ann Robertson, the woman who put John and Keith up last night, who is a teacher and also a member of the SWP. The hall was packed and there must have been at least a thousand people inside which made me a bit weak at the knees. We made our way down to the front and sat down as the speakers on the platform began urging such 'radical' actions as one day strikes and going to arbitration, and these were the educated elite! No one was calling for all out strike action which seemed to me, an ignorant miner, the obvious course of action because with us already out the Tories wouldn't relish a fight against two powerful unions.

A motion was put that a striking miner be allowed to address the meeting and after being seconded a vote was taken. To my disappointment, and a bit of relief, the motion didn't get the two thirds majority needed but it was close apparently and that was encouraging. I momentarily considered storming the stage and speaking anyway but I couldn't buck up the courage. When a young man took the microphone and introduced himself as a Christian teacher and then began quoting passages from the

Bible that proved that strikes were evil I decided there was no point in me staying so I left the hall.

Back outside I stood collecting with a bucket and was really pleased by the response I got as the teachers left the hall, with some of them stopping to say they wished I'd been given a chance to speak. Irene told them a meeting was being held in a nearby pub at 12.30 and that I would be speaking there and all were welcome. We set off with me carrying the bucket, which was gratifyingly full and arm achingly heavy.

Inside the pub I met Gary, who had also not had the chance to speak, though he has been invited back tomorrow when he's been assured he will be allowed to speak. There were about 30 people at the meeting and both Gary and myself spoke briefly before answering the usual questions, such as, 'Why hasn't there been a national ballot'? and, 'Why should the miners be exempt from job losses?' My response to the first question was that we had all been allowed a democratic vote in our own areas, with everyone being given the opportunity to voice their opinion. The result is that the majority of NUM members are now out on strike, and because we are the majority the areas that are scabbing should join us because the majority should rule. As for job losses miners have always suffered from jobs being lost. In Durham alone 80,000 jobs have gone since nationalisation in 1947 when the industry was supposedly given to the people. We got a good round of applause and received another £20, which added to the morning's collection made a total of £74.82p. Gary is really impressed with both the organisational abilities of the SWP and their politics and agreed to speak to a meeting in the evening in the same pub.

After the meeting Gary and me went with a comrade called Dick to a picket of Johnsons Paints where the workers have been out for 2 weeks in pursuance of a pay claim. It was interesting talking to the 5 pickets and swapping experiences but I got the impression that they weren't too interested in what we had to say. We left after half an hour, mainly because it was bloody freezing but also because we had to collect our stuff from Hilary's because her mother had arrived.

Dick drove us and he was a mine of knowledge about Manchester's history, especially Peterloo. We thanked him for his trouble and the history lesson.

We met up with John and Keith who told us the morning picket at Agecroft had been boring and we hadn't missed anything. I asked them if they wanted to come along to an SWP meeting and at first they didn't seem keen but when I told them the meeting was held in a pub they agreed.

It was agreed that Keith would go to Central branch with Gary, and John would come with me to Salford branch. We would all meet up at our new lodgings later. We packed our bags and I put the silver and copper into the bottom of my holdall which made it very heavy. Ann picked us up at 7.15 and we drove the short distance to the pub and parked the car outside. Hilary drove Gary and Keith to Central branch and then returned to our meeting because it's her branch.

The meeting was excellent with a full room to hear Roger Cox, a comrade from London, speak. We had an excellent discussion on the strike and my contribution was well received. I tried to encourage John to speak but he was too shy but still seemed to enjoy the debate, though he was a bit put out by the criticism of Scargill. In the break I tried to explain to John that no one was above criticism, even if they are vastly superior to your average trade union leader. John remained unconvinced. The rest of the meeting went well and I was given a lot of envelopes by comrades containing money they had collected.

I felt elated at the money we had got for the Women's Support Group but it was short lived because when we got to Ann's car we found the back windows had been smashed and our bags were gone! I'd lost all my clothes, my glasses and all the coins collected this morning. Fortunately the notes were safely in my pocket. John hadn't been daft enough to leave money in his bag but he also lost his clothes, and more importantly to him, he'd lost the diary he'd been keeping for his kids when they grew up. Mine was in my pocket. We cursed our stupidity at leaving our bags in the car in the first place but there's no point crying over spilt milk. We did a quick scout around the area to see if our bags had been ditched but had no luck. I asked some kids if they'd seen anything but just got blank stares in response. Little bastards!

Back at the car Ann was upset about the damage to her car and wondered what she should do. We went back into the pub and they had a whip round which raised £20. I offered John half but he refused and said he still had £30 in his pocket, which was kind of him. Ann was advised to report the theft and damage to the police even though we knew they wouldn't do anything. The main reason was so Ann could claim from her insurance so we drove the short distance to the cop shop to make our report. A bored pig went through his routine and only perked up a bit when we gave our addresses and asked what we were doing in Manchester. We of course lied and said we were just visiting friends but he gave us both a shock by saying he was sure he'd seen us somewhere before, but we assured him that was impossible as we'd only just arrived this evening. Agecroft isn't far away and he could possibly have seen us but I doubt it. Bastard was just testing us out. He told us it was highly unlikely they'd catch anyone but said they'd contact us if they did.

Anne drove us slowly to Prestwich to Geoff Brown's house and I apologised to her because I felt it was the sight of our bags that had caused the break in. She told me to forget it and put it down to experience.

We were given a warm welcome by our new hosts, Geoff and Julie.

They were very sympathetic when they heard about the theft and gave us tea and homemade cake. John was miserable as sin, and as soon as his mate arrived they went to their room. Gary and I chatted about our meetings and I wasn't too surprised when Gary told me that a committee man from Easington had spoken like an idiot, extolling the great virtues of Scargill and how we all had to do what he said as if he was some kind of god, and he took all the collection for union funds. To be fair, I know a lot of the lads from Easington and they are excellent so perhaps this man was having a bad night, and I know the money will be well used. Gary did manage to speak and was pleased at the reception he received. His confidence is growing, which is great.

Our room is great and we both have a comfortable bed to sleep in. as usual Gary is snoring soundly and I'm about to join him. The only clothes I have left are at the side of the bed, a pair of jeans, a shirt, pair of underpants, socks, boots, jacket and coat.

Thursday May 10th, 1984

Gary eventually managed to wake me at 5.15 after I had slept through an alarm clock and a radio switched on next to my bed. Gary had taken a shower before I managed to drag myself off to the bathroom, skipping the shower in favour of a wash with ice cold water to wake me up.

Downstairs we found Geoff had got up before us and made breakfast, eggs on toast and hot strong coffee. Lovely. He drove the four of us to the picket line at Agecroft with John and Keith almost silent, though I put this down to the events of last night. There was only Stan the local nutter and another couple of local pickets when we arrived, but the rest of the lads arrived shortly after us. They told us that we weren't going home today as had been planned but were going home tomorrow instead. We were all to be given an extra £8 but anyone who wanted to go as planned could do so because a coach was leaving straight after the picket. I'm glad to report that only a handful of the older men left, with most of us looking forward to spending our few quid.

Geoff left at seven to get ready for work. He is a lecturer in Trade Union Studies at Manchester Poly and he asked if Gary and myself could call in to see him at eleven because he wanted us to speak to his class of shop stewards. Just after Geoff left a taxi sped past us and into the pit. I said to Gary that the scabs must be making good money to be able to afford taxis into work but he said the scabs weren't paying for it, Thatcher is. I agreed until one of the lads told us it wasn't scabs in the taxi–it was some pickets from Wearmouth who were going to storm into the canteen and get the scabs! I admired their guts but feared for their safety.

Ten minutes later the lads were marched out through the gates by an escort of pigs and to our loud cheers they were allowed to rejoin the picket. Apparently they ran into the canteen only to find it full of pigs who stared at them in amazement before they were nicked. They said they couldn't understand why they hadn't been arrested but weren't complaining. Personally I think the police admired their bloody cheek, and anyway, they hadn't actually committed a crime.

After all the scabs went in Gary and I walked to a nearby shop to get chocolate for him and fags for me, and when we got back we found most of the lads had gone, with only about a dozen left. They told us the coach was coming back for us so we stood about chatting, guarded by two bored pigs who had probably drawn the short straws. As we talked a really flash car approached the entrance and I shouted SCAB at the top of my voice, making a couple of lads jump. To my great surprise the car screeched to a halt and a huge pig got out, ramming a swagger stick beneath his arm, and began to stride across the road towards us with a look on his face that said he wasn't amused. He was a huge bastard, brick shithouse like, with a bright red face. I thought I was in for it but instead he headed to a Westoe picket known as 'Vic the Brick' and accused him of the shouting. Vic rightfully denied being responsible but the pig called him a liar and started to poke him in the chest with his stick saying, 'Why don't you take these other vermin back to Durham where you crawled from?' Vic is not the sort of lad to take that from anyone, not even by a very senior policeman, and replied, 'If you touch me with that fuckin' stick once more I'll wrap it round your fat fuckin' neck!' The pig took Vic's advice about the stick but shouted for his henchmen to clear the area immediately. He looked like he was about to explode, like one of those cartoon characters who eat something too hot. Pigs came running from the canteen and began to force us away by pushing us down the road, with us being as difficult as possible but stopping short of being arrested. One pig told us to be careful because that was James Anderton, Chief Constable of Manchester. Vic still wasn't impressed!

On the coach I got another shock when a committee man from Wearmouth came storming up and demanded that John be given £30 to compensate for his bag. I was totally gobsmacked and said I didn't have £30. The only money I had was the money collected for our Women's Support Group who badly needed funds. He said the SWP had given me money, and if they could give me money, they could give John money as well. I told him John had refused to accept his half, and it was only £20 collected which wouldn't even replace my clothes. He then said we should put it to the vote, telling everyone I was trying to undermine the union. I gave in and handed the Judas his thirty pieces of silver. The bastard couldn't even look me in the eye, and even had the cheek to ask if I could bring Keith's and his fuckin' bags to the picket line in the morning because they had found somewhere else to stay! Gary wanted to punch him but I said it wouldn't help. The whole thing left me feeling like shit and yet again I'm accused of something I never did by petty officials. Bastards!

At the Poly we were met by Phil who had a full day planned for us but we were glad of the chance to do something positive. We agreed to meet outside Piccadilly train station at 12 and then set off to find Geoff's office.

After a few wrong turnings we managed to find it in an annexe at the back of the Poly. We were asked to wait whilst Geoff went to ask his class if they wanted to let us speak. We chatted with his secretary and she asked if we were working miners or striking miners and, were we Geordies? I said yes but ones with brains who supported Sunderland. She supports Man City and we chatted nicely for ten minutes or so about football, especially Bobby Charlton and the merits of individual skills in football.

Geoff returned to tell us his class had voted to let us speak and asked the secretary if she'd like to come along. She agreed but said she only had a few minutes to spare because she was very busy. Gary confessed to being as nervous as hell but I told him I was the same and we'd manage fine. There were about twenty students present plus another lecturer, Geoff and the secretary. Geoff introduced us and I started by giving a brief outline of how the strike had started, with Gary elaborating on what I said before we both settled to answer questions. The questions were predictable, ballot, scabs, violence, policing and flying pickets, and we answered all of them, taking turns at answering. I think we did well because they had a collection which raised £40, including a quid from the secretary who had stayed till the end. Geoff later told us she was a Tory and had initially refused to even meet us, so it just goes to show how ideas can be changed through argument.

We had a coffee with some of the students afterwards and discovered one of them was a bus driver and shop steward at a local depot. I told him about the buses going into Agecroft and he went straight to a phone to have it stopped, so that was a bonus. We told Geoff we'd see him about five and also told him that the Judas's wouldn't be coming back. This surprised him as well but he told us not to be bitter because they were only doing what most people do, looking after number one.

Gary was elated at our success and for the first time said he was seriously considering joining the SWP. At the Railway Club we spoke to about 30 men at an unofficial meeting because the stewards had refused to call a special meeting. I let Gary do most of the talking and he urged the rail workers to come out in support of the NUM and that overtime bans and one day strikes were not enough. United action would really give the Tories a fight. He got a great reception and we were handed £120 which they'd collected. Again Gary was full of confidence as we left the meeting.

We had a bit of time to spare before we met Phil so we went to a nearby market where I bought a cheap bag, three pairs of underpants for a quid and some socks for the same price, and two sweatshirts for £2 each, all out of my £8 picket money.

Phil drove us to his flat for a quick cup of coffee and introduced us to a couple of lads from Davey Hulme Waterworks who were to take us to a meeting outside the gates. The lads were brilliant, like a comedy duo, cracking jokes all the way, with one of them bearing a strong resemblance to Mike Harding, the folk singer. The 'waterworks' was really a sewage plant and the smell was awful but we soon had about 20 men waiting to hear us. Again all the usual questions were asked and answered, with one man standing out and asking most of the questions. He had a copy of the *Sun* sticking out of his pocket and he seemed amazed when he heard that the average striking miner and his family were living on £12 a week from Social Insecurity plus family allowance, whilst single miners received nothing at all! A union official told us he was surprised that we were in the area to picket Agecroft because when they had a strike the Agecroft men gave them financial support and stood on their picket lines! He has agreed to try and join our picket in the morning.

As we were leaving the union man gave us £20 which had been collected but more impressively the *Sun* reader shook my hand and as he walked off I found a ten quid note in my hand! That really made our day!

Before we went back to Geoff's we attended a student meeting at Manchester University and yet again answered all the usual questions about ballots etc, but at least we are learning how to convince people with rock solid arguments.

Back at Geoff's we took a much needed shower and then ate a lovely meal which Geoff had cooked. The best I can manage is egg and chips! We had a really interesting conversation about the SWP and Geoff told us he had spent some time in Germany and was active in their equivalent of the SWP. I bet he's an excellent lecturer.

Phil picked us up at 7.30 to go to Gorton branch meeting, held in an upstairs room in a pub. This was the best meeting I've been to so far and the main speaker was excellent, John Taylor from Bradford who spoke on 'The History of the Labour Party'. It was very interesting and he made it better by adding a lot of humour. Gary and I did our bit but this time stressed the role the SWP played for us as miners and how we worked in the strike. We had a good time, and for once we got pissed. Again I was given a load of envelopes containing money collected by comrades.

Friday May 11th, 1984

Julie drove us to the picket line this morning because Geoff was knackered. She is a teacher but still managed to stay for an hour before going to work. Again we arrived before the majority of pickets so I grabbed the chance to stand right outside the gate as one of the six 'official' pickets. Gary stood with Julie across the road. As the scabs began to arrive we tried flagging them down but not one of them would stop. Two of the lads were from Agecroft and have been out on strike since day one. If it's hard for us then how much tougher must it be for them? One lad was forced to go back across the road for the unforgivable crime of shouting 'Scab', and I wasn't long after him after posing with a limp wrist and pouting. Julie said I was being sexist and I couldn't argue. I was just trying to wind them up but her point was taken.

Stanley outdid himself today. He had constructed a shrine on the pavement consisting of a picture of a policeman surrounded by triangular pieces of silver paper, with a cross and a dead sparrow completing the thing. Stan danced around his shrine chanting curses against the police, stopping every now and again to talk into his coat collar, saying things like,'3,000 pickets arriving in 10 minutes, over', shouting in a loud voice for the benefit of the bemused pigs. After a while the pigs came over and destroyed Stan's subversive shrine, causing the liveliest reaction of the morning from the pickets, but this was only loud boos and jeering. The picket ended, and after we had thrown John and Keith's bags at them we headed off to Manchester Poly.

Gary and I did a paper sale and managed to sell half a dozen copies. We were disgusted when we were talking to a young lass from Sunderland and some of our pickets started shouting at her, asking her to 'get her tits out for the lads'. We shouted back at the lads and told them not to be so bloody stupid and sexist. All this achieved was to enhance our reputation as 'snobby bastards'.

One of the Westoe lads told us there was to be a meeting to discuss whether we should stay an extra day so we can attend a rally in St.Helen's tomorrow. After a short meeting at which the main issue seemed to be whether we would get an extra £8, it was agreed that we will attend the rally. Gary and I rang home to tell our wives and received a right ear bashing! Kath was really pissed off and suggested I should just stay away if I was enjoying myself so much. She isn't happy at all and wouldn't listen to my explanations. Gary got much the same from his wife so we retreated to a nearby café for a coffee and clear our ears. The café was owned by a Greek Cypriot who supports the strike and we had a fascinating half hour listening to tales of his struggles back home in Cyprus. He also said that Reagan is an imbecile and that the USA are the biggest threat to world peace. We reluctantly left because we had another meeting to attend and Phil was waiting outside.

The meeting was in the Armstrong Hall in Salford, and like its namesake in South Shields sold Vaux beer, which Gary calls 'gnats piss'. Phil told us we were to speak to Probation Officers and neither of us was expecting much of a reception. How wrong we were. We spoke to about 30 people and concentrated on how the law was being deliberately misused to break the strike, how the violence mainly came from the police, and how the bail conditions imposed on arrested men were completely out of proportion to the mainly trivial offences. We got a standing ovation and received £80 from the collection taken. It was brilliant and for me the highlight of our visit.

Back at Geoff's we counted up all the money collected and were amazed to find we have £411.23p, which will really help the Women's Support Group, and keep the pie run going. We are going for a final night out with the Manchester comrades but this time we'll leave the money at home!

Saturday May 12th, 1984

Geoff drove us to the Greenbank Club where we'd been told to report for 9am. We said our grateful thanks to Geoff and Julie for their hospitality and went into the club. Nine'o'clock came and went and it wasn't until 9.40 that the coach finally arrived. I had a furious row with our union man for making us wait because he'd told the driver to arrive at 9.30.

The rally in St.Helen's was massive with well over 10,000 attending. All the Durham Area Lodge banners had been brought through on the Executive coach along with most of the Executive led by Tommy Callan and Harold Mitchell. Every pit in Durham and Northumberland was represented.

We set off at 11.30 and it took ages to march along the route. Just as we were about to get to the place where the speeches were to be made our committee men ordered us all to get on the coach and that anyone who didn't would be left. I tried to argue that we'd each been given £8 to attend and the least we could do was listen to a few speeches. They ignored me and our coach left, leaving at least a couple of lads behind. Nobody seemed bothered.

On the way back the Wearmouth committee man again tried to turn the men against me, saying I was more interested in selling 'commie' papers than being a picket, and demanded I share out all the money collected between the 4 Lodges on the coach. There was no way I was going to do that after all the hard work Gary and me had put in whilst a lot of them were getting pissed. I told him we'd given the money back rather than share it with useless twats like him! If he wasn't against me before he certainly is now and I shall have to be more careful from now on. It's bad enough having the full force of the state against us without my own side joining in. They make me sick!

Kath is furious and refuses to even talk to me, especially as Mick Armstrong from Newcastle SWP has just phoned and told me a coach is leaving South Shields at 8am to attend a rally in Mansfield. I told Kath I'll be going so she's gone to bed in a foul mood, but not until she called me a selfish bastard. I do see her point but what can I do? The sooner we win this strike the sooner we can get back to normal.

Monday May 14th, 1984

Today has been the most frustrating and disappointing day of the strike so far, and also the most violent!

Scargill had called for a mass demonstration in Mansfield to show the strength of the strike, and to show support for the 11,000 Notts men on strike with us. Our Lodge officials responded by providing ONE coach, leaving a lot of the regular pickets disappointed. Fortunately Ian Wilburn had helped to organise a coach through Newcastle SWP to show our Lodge officials they weren't the only ones who could organise and that the SWP weren't only interested in selling papers.

There were 15 of us and the bus turned up late so we didn't have time to get more lads for the bus, which was disappointing. The men on the union coach were each paid £5 to keep them during the day so we decided to do the same out of the money collected in Manchester, and to try and claim it back off the Lodge later. We caught up with the Newcastle Poly bus at a service station and that was full, but Simon, the organiser, was having trouble getting the Labour Party and *Militant* members on board to contribute towards the cost of our coach. We also offered to pay for that but Simon refused and said he would sort it out.

We arrived in Mansfield at 11am and told the driver to return at 4pm. The rally was to start from a community centre and return there for the rally after we'd marched through the streets of Mansfield. The car park of the centre was jam packed with dozens of colourful banners and we pushed our way through to our Lodge banner. There were a lot of surprised faces amongst the Westoe men when we showed up. I was shocked when Tommy Wilson and the lads gathered round him threatened to beat up Ian Wilburn and Keith Smoult! They said nothing to me but there was a really nasty atmosphere and I warned Ian and Keith to keep away from Tommy and his henchmen. The only reason I can think of for Tommy's attitude is he's a committee man and perhaps felt he was being undermined in some way.

The march set off and was a wonderful sight, with 'Victory to the Miners' placards everywhere. Ian, Keith and myself kept to the edge of the march so we could try and sell papers and pretty soon I had sold all the papers I had. One thing that was very noticeable was the low profile of the pigs, though there were helicopters constantly buzzing overhead. I felt tremendously proud as we marched through the crowded streets of Mansfield and felt that such a display of solidarity couldn't be ignored by the Notts scabs. My pride soon turned to embarrassment as the miners began to chant, 'Get your tits out for the lads, tits out for the lads', in response to a some young shop girls leaning out of an upstairs window. To make it worse we were directly behind a Women's Support Group from Yorkshire! I shouted at lads to stop but only got called 'puff' and 'queer' in response. One lad said it was only a bit of fun, a laugh, and anyway the lasses liked it. They just couldn't see anything wrong with their behaviour but how can we expect women to support us when we just treat them with such disrespect? I was relieved when the chant changed to, 'Piggy, piggy, piggy, oink, oink, oink,' a variation on the 'Maggie' chant. At least that was aimed at an enemy.

As we returned to the car park I decided to stay at the entrance to see if I could see any familiar faces. It was wonderful to see all the different groups and banners and I felt very encouraged. As I was standing a young woman approached me and asked if I would like to buy a copy of her paper, *The Next Step*, which I knew was the paper of the Revolutionary Communist Party. When I looked at the front cover I was shocked to see the headline calling for a national ballot to unite the miners. I told her she should join *Militant*, or the Tory party but she continued to argue that a ballot was the only way to unite the miners. I told her we are united and couldn't she see that? The scabs are a minority and a ballot would only divide us further, but she went on and on about ballots till I lost my temper and told her to go away, though I used more colourful language! I'm sure RCP stands for the Ray Chadburn Party.

I was saved by the appearance of Phil Ramsall and Irene Davis from Manchester and we stood discussing the possibility of a mass picket which we felt was the real reason for the rally. As the speeches began we stood gobsmacked as Scargill introduced Tony Benn as 'The greatest Energy Minister we have ever had'. I couldn't believe my ears because it was Benn who had introduced the divisive Incentive Scheme, despite a national ballot rejecting it two to one. In my opinion it is the Incentive Scheme which has caused the Notts miners to scab, because whilst they can earn huge bonuses in their nice thick seams, we only get a pittance in our thin seams under the North Sea, so they have a lot more money to lose than we have. To me he is the perfect example to all those misguided left wingers who believe that all we have to do is vote in a few hundred MPs like him and we'll have Socialism. Bollocks!! We waited for Scargill and were really disappointed to hear no more than his usual stirring rhetoric, but no call for mass picketing, so we headed to a nearby pub for some dinner. We had fish and chips and a pint before Phil and Irene left, and I returned to the car park to find the lads.

I met up with some of the students from Newcastle and we headed for the same nearby pub to pass the time before our coaches returned. There were some Westoe lads already in there and we joined them. Two of the students, Brenda and Joan, turned the discussion to the sexist chants and said they were 'fucking disgusting and fucking demeaning'. One of the

Top: Norman (centre) during the strike
Above: Miners picket a power station
Right: Women supporters of the strike
Below: Scab bus

PICTURES: JOHN STURROCK/NORMAN STRIKE (TOP)

"Like a scene from the English Civil War!"
Police confront pickets at Orgreave coking plant near Birmingham

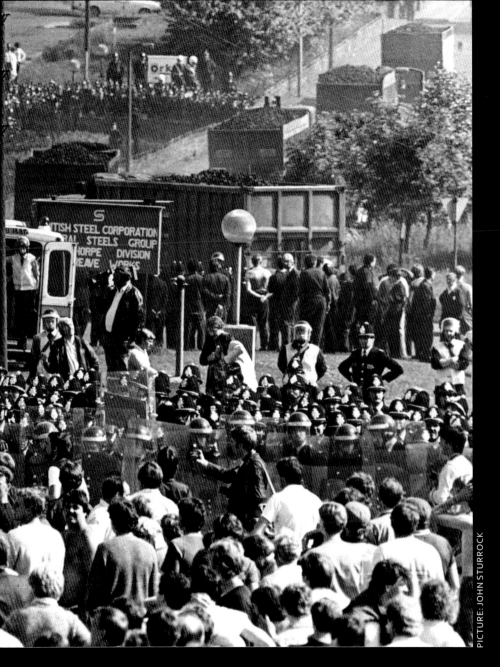

"it was the fight of our lives. The way we stood up for what we believed in took everyone by surprise"

PICTURES: JOHN STURROCK

lads said, 'If you were my wife I'd give you a good hiding for using foul language like that!' I tried to diffuse the situation by chipping in with, 'How would you feel if I asked your wife or daughter to get their tits out?' One of the lads jumped up, really offended, and Brenda jumped up, even more offended, but thankfully the landlord called 'Time' and ordered us all out. In the bogs we heard some lads saying that Scargill had done a deal with the pigs that allowed the rally to go ahead in exchange for no picketing. I just didn't want to believe that one but it did explain the low police presence and the absence of a call for mass picketing. The news had reported that there were 40,000 people present at the rally, and the police could never have prevented that many people from picketing. To me it seemed like a lost opportunity.

We left the pub, strolling towards the car park and enjoying the sunshine. Suddenly we jumped at the sound of breaking glass and saw a mob of policemen in full riot gear appear from behind the community centre and set about two lads, kicking and punching them. We all started shouting and running towards the lads to help them when all of a sudden police on huge horses started coming out of the community centre and broke into a gallop, clubbing people as they came. I was momentarily frozen but the sight of a man falling to the ground with blood pouring from his head shook me to life and I started to run towards a church doorway across a road, I remember thinking that they couldn't touch me there. People were screaming and shouting and running in all directions to avoid the horses. I watched in shock from the church doorway as a woman with a pushchair was knocked to the ground and her child fell over, screaming loudly. Not one of the pigs running in the wake of the horses stopped to help her or the child, too intent on clubbing anyone they could get their hands on. They were dressed all in black with crash helmets, plastic shields and truncheons, and after they had passed, I ran out and helped her and the child to the doorway, then ran out again to help a man covered in blood get to safety. The pigs were just going berserk, out of control. I remember thinking of Peterloo, only it was batons instead of sabres!

Eventually we made our way back to the car park where coaches were constantly moving out. I spotted some familiar faces and ran to join them. I was told the pigs had ordered everyone to leave by 3.30pm and that anyone remaining after that would be arrested and charged with rioting! Someone had been sent to try and find our coach whilst our group grew by the minute as people returned in ones and two's, each with their own horror stories to tell. Pigs were everywhere, shouting at people to leave and making arrests for no apparent reason. We were very relieved when our coach arrived and the pigs started to shove us roughly on board. We did a head count and no one was missing and we let loads of Yorkshire pickets from Doncaster get on our coach because theirs had been forced to leave. One lad had to hide under the back seat because the pigs were after him and we all breathed a huge sigh of relief as we left Mansfield behind and got back onto the M1.

I was talking to one of the Yorkshire lads and he told me his version of what had happened. Apparently a lad had been wearing a toy cop's hat and the pigs just attacked him, causing his mates to retaliate by throwing stuff at them. That's when riot police DID come streaming out of the Community Centre followed by the horses. A real life Trojan horse.

A cynic might say that because this all happened just as the pubs closed the pigs could justify their actions by blaming 'drunken hooligans' who left them no option but to respond as they had, and then make an example of those arrested so that others would be discouraged from coming to Notts. Another cynic might ask what all those pigs and horses were doing in a Community Centre. Marx said, 'Political power is the organised power of one class for oppressing another.' It's about time we started oppressing them for a change!!

Friday May 18th, 1984

The days since Mansfield have been boring because my ban from Tow Law has meant I've had to go to Lumley No 6 pit instead. Despite its name it's no longer a colliery but a site where coal from open cast sites is cleaned and sorted.

Each day there have been about 70 pickets present, mostly lads like myself who have been banned from Tow Law. Lorries arrive 12 at a time at around 9.30 each day but no attempt is made to stop them. We just shout 'Scab' at them because we are greatly outnumbered by the pigs. It's so disheartening, and even when the pigs provoke us no one has the confidence to fight back. Like on Wednesday when a pig took offence at the 'Stop the Police State' placards we had placed along the fence opposite the site. Some of the older men actually told the pig he was right whilst the rest of us just glared at them. It is that frustrating I'm starting to wonder if there's any point and that I should just stay at home. I suppose the reason I won't is that there are a few younger lads who I can talk to and try to agitate for switching the picket to the steelworks on Teesside.

Tonight the Lodge Secretary, Walter Slater, reimbursed me for the money we spent on the trip to Mansfield, £65, and told me not to organise any more trips because the Lodge can't afford it! A load of bollocks!

After talking with some of the lads I've taken round a petition which demands that a union meeting be held. We haven't had one for weeks because the officials say they have nothing to say. Well, we'll have plenty to fuckin' say, especially about picketing. The majority of men I spoke to have signed the petition and I went to hand it to one of the committee men. I also managed to sell 37 copies of *Socialist Worker* which shows that at least the rank and file are prepared to take on board new ideas.

Unfortunately Ian Wilburn hasn't been seen since Mansfield and I fear the threats made against him there have put him off. It's a bloody shame!

Monday May 21st, 1984

I decided to try picketing at Woodside Drift Mine near Consett in the hope it would be more inspiring than Lumley. It wasn't but it did give me the opportunity to talk to a few more Westoe men and agitate for the union meeting which is to be held on Wednesday morning. I also spoke to a lot of the pickets before they left for Tow Law, and it looks like the resolutions I intend to propose will be passed because they are what the men want. They are:

1. Weekly union meetings.
2. Setting up a kitchen in the Armstrong Hall.
3. A cooker to be bought for the Women's Support Group.
4. More pickets to travel away.
5. The Women's Support Group to be helped financially by the Lodge.
6. A strike committee to be elected.
7. Pickets to be sent to the steelworks on Teesside.

The Women's Support Group is going very well, despite the positive animosity and unhelpful attitude of our Lodge officials, hence the resolutions. The women have set up an office in the National Union of Seamen's premises in Coronation Street, South Shields, and it's from there they are distributing food parcels. Gary Marshall and me went down to see them and gave them £300 from what we collected in Manchester, keeping the rest in reserve in case we need it. We offered to help out but the women refused, saying they want to stay independent. Fair enough.

Kath has been promoted to Warden of the Women's Aid Refuge due to her boss taking a six months leave of absence. It means a slight pay rise, a lot more responsibility, and the chance of a permanent job if the other woman doesn't come back. It also takes the pressure off me because she is a lot happier.

Wednesday May 23rd, 1984

I am absolutely shattered, depressed and disillusioned, though not as much as I was after this morning's union meeting, thanks to comrades rallying around me at our SWP branch meeting this evening.

I had arrived at the Armstrong Hall full of confidence after doing the early morning picket at Woodside. I was determined that the men would show their disgust at how the officials were running the strike. The hall was full and I sat in the middle with Gary and Keith, preparing myself for a blistering attack against the platform.

The minutes of the previous meeting were read out and passed, then Walter Slater stood up to read the correspondence. The first thing he said was how shocked and disgusted he was about a letter he'd received from Parsons which revealed they'd had a letter from him appealing for money. He said he had never written to Parsons yet this letter was signed by him so it was obviously a forgery. The letter went on to complain about the behaviour of Norman Strike who had insulted the Secretary at Parsons and taken an unofficial collection. Slater said he had always trusted me and asked if I was in the meeting. The bastard knew I was because he could plainly see me. I stood up and my legs were shaking and everyone turned to stare at me. He stuck the knife in firmly by saying that in all his years of union activity he had never been so shocked and disgusted by one of his members doing such a wicked thing. He asked me if I had committed the forgery or was it someone else ?

I tried to defend myself against the implication that I had tried to get money for myself but I wasn't allowed to say anything other than admit I had written his name on the letter. Tommy Wilson then stood and launched a personal attack against my character, calling the SWP a bunch of 'tin pot communists' and openly accused me of forging the letter to raise funds for them. I was shocked and stunned as more people stood up and joined the attack, calling for me to be dealt with harshly as an example to anyone else who might 'wish to profit from the strike'. I was given the chance to explain myself but I was so upset and shocked I couldn't express myself clearly, and even my mates didn't look convinced. John Chapman, the Chairman, then asked that the Lodge Committee be allowed to deal with me as they saw fit and this was agreed by a unanimous show of hands.

I felt awful and wanted the floor to open up and swallow me as men looked at me with utter contempt. Gary and Keith tried to console me but even they didn't sound convinced so I left to hisses and went home on my own, thoroughly depressed.

At home my shame turned to anger and I vowed to pack it all in and just stay at home. Ungrateful bastards! Every penny I have collected has always been witnessed and accounted for, and the supposed forgery wasn't even an attempt at forgery because it bore no resemblance to Slater's real signature, and the letter itself was the one I had got from Wearmouth which I'd photocopied with our Lodge heading instead of Wearmouths, and I'd signed Slater's name at the bottom where Dave Hopper's had been. The only address was that of the Lodge, not mine, so how could I possibly profit from it? I have other questions now. Why has it taken almost 5 weeks for the 'forgery' to come to light? How long has Slater had it? Why wait until now if what I'm alleged to have done is so serious? I will have to ask these questions when I appear in front of the committee, whenever that is.

I had quite a few phone calls from comrades urging me to attend tonight's branch meeting so I went. I'm pleased I did because it's put everything into perspective. Comrades convinced me that giving up and staying at home would be a bad move because it would only serve to prove my 'guilt' in the eyes of the pickets. They're right. They also think this was a deliberate ploy by the Lodge because I am a thorn in their sides and they want to get rid of me. Makes sense so I will continue, though the whole thing has left a very bitter taste in my mouth!

Kath has been excellent and is also very angry at what has happened. She has also urged me to continue, which is brilliant.

The NUM met MacGregor for talks today but they broke down after just an hour. What a surpise!

Friday May 25th, 1984

I went for picketing this morning and I managed to speak to lads outside the Armstrong Hall explaining exactly what I had done, and when I'd done it, and asked the questions such as why has it taken the Lodge so long to accuse me if what I did was as serious as had been said? I got a sympathetic hearing there, and on the picket at Woodside Drift mine in the morning. Mind you Tommy Wilson saw me talking to the lads and actually threatened to 'kick my commie head in' and told them not to believe a word I said because I am a 'fuckin' lying bastard'. He is one scary man and I want to keep as far away from him as possible because I believe he will carry out his threats if I give him the chance!

I still tried to sell *Socialist Worker* but no one was buying. I'll just have to keep on trying.

Monday May 28th, 1984

Back at Woodside and the usual boring picket, nothing happening. The lads are all talking about what is happening down at Orgreave in Yorkshire where mass pickets are taking place. Why aren't we down there as well instead of wasting our time here? Problem is that all I can do is agitate amongst the pickets. I can't confront the officials directly because of my being under suspicion. The good thing is that the pickets seem to believe my explanations so hopefully no further action will happen.

Wednesday May 30th, 1984

Woodside again and no action at all. There was a major confrontation at Orgreave where thousands of police have been battling with pickets. There were dozens of arrests, including Scargill, and loads of pickets injured. No matter what people may say about Scargill he is without doubt the best trade union leader going. I can't think of any other leader who would even go on a picket, let alone get arrested alongside his men.

Why the hell aren't we down there? What the hell are our leaders doing letting the Yorkshire lads fight alone when we waste our time on stupid drift mines? One thing is certain and that is we can't win this strike unless we all stick together!

Wednesday June 6th, 1984

I've spent the last week picketing at Woodside. I say picketing but we never, ever see anyone to picket. I think they just send us here to get us out of the way because most of us have been banned from Tow Law. I'm up in court tomorrow and hopefully will be free to return to Tow Law once we've been dealt with. We just spend our time playing football or walking through the woods and enjoying the warm sunshine. To be honest, it's nice getting a tan and breathing fresh air and I've decided that win or lose I am NOT ever going back down the pit. I haven't told Kath and don't intend to until the strike is settled. I'll find a job somewhere. We are managing OK on Kath's wages so I can afford to take a job that pays less than being a miner.

Last week there was a picket of the Orgreave coke works in Yorkshire and there was a lot of violence, with 82 arrests, and a lot of lads injured. Why weren't we there instead of wasting our bloody time here?

FRUSTRATION

Thursday June 7th, 1984
Today has been a huge disappointment in terms of solidarity and as a result I have had my first ever experience of prison, though only for a few hours.

Sixty eight of us appeared at Bishop Auckland Magistrates Court to answer charges relating to picketing at Tow Law over the past two months. The first cases to be heard were those men arrested at Deerness with the MP Bob Clay in April. Deerness is an entrance to the open cast site at Tow Law. I was arrested at Inkerman, which is another entrance to the same site, which is huge.

Twelve men faced the bench, and when the first of them was again remanded on bail it was discovered that that the bail conditions had been changed. They had been; 'Not to go within two miles of Deerness'. Now it was: 'Not to go within a two mile radius of Tow Law'. This small change meant the lads would no longer be able to picket at Inkerman as they had been because it was just over two miles from Deerness, but not from Tow Law. The change caused uproar in the court and the magistrate adjourned the proceedings for 15 minutes to allow the men to consult with their solicitor.

We held a mass meeting outside to decide what to do because six of the lads said they were going to refuse the new conditions. After a lot of debate and a warning from the solicitor that refusal meant prison, it was agreed that we should all stand together. If one man went to prison then we would all go to prison. We piled into the courtroom to take our stand.

Frank Duffy from Murton Colliery was first up and he refused the conditions, saying, 'I can't accept this. I'd rather be locked up.' The female magistrate sentenced him to seven days remand in Durham Prison and he was led down to huge applause from the pickets. He was closely followed by five others, including John Humble and Keith Smoult from Westoe. Unfortunately the other 6 lads lacked the courage and accepted the conditions. One of these was a committee man from Westoe who said he was 'more valuable outside'. That's a bloody laugh! Another Westoe lad, Steve Oliver, tried to refuse but the magistrate told him his bail was unconditional so he had nothing to refuse. This gave us a bit of light relief. After that the rot set in and man after man accepted the bail conditions. I was determined to stick with my principles and go to jail, hoping it would get the planned protest back on track.

My name was called and I stood in front of the magistrate and was charged with Obstruction of the Highway with exactly the same bail conditions as I'd previously accepted. My response was to say, 'I refuse to accept these conditions on the grounds that they are an infringement upon my civil liberties and are a block on my ability to travel at will in a free country.' This was met with cheers of encouragement from the lads but pissed off the magistrate who threatened to have the court cleared. She advised me to reconsider my decision and consult with my solicitor. I refused and she said that as that was the case she had no alternative but to have me remanded in custody for 7 days and I was led down. I went with my arm raised and my fist clenched with all the pickets cheering.

There were dozens of police beneath the court, obviously expecting trouble. I was searched and relieved of my few possessions and then put into a cell with the six lads already sent down. They asked where everyone else was and I had to tell them it looked as if the whole protest was going to be a flop. We sat around the cell expressing our anger and frustration at the empty words of our mates. Only one more lad had the guts to join us and he told us the court had been cleared and no one else was coming. He also told us that one of the most vociferous supporters of mass action, a Wearmouth picket called Bob Robson, had phoned Tyne Tees Television and told them to come down and get a scoop. He also excused himself from the protest because he has a wife and two kids. That made us all so angry because we all had families but we'd agreed to make a stand. If we'd all stood together what could they have done? We'll never know.

Our solicitor came down and begged us to reverse our decision, but we all refused and told him he was useless. He left in a huff and the next to try was one of the Durham Area Executives. He said he could understand the other 6 because their bail conditions had changed, but me and the other lad were just being stupid. Frank Duffy said it was a pity the other 60 lads hadn't been as stupid and we could have won a victory. He also left and we settled down to wait.

We were all handcuffed then put into one of them long vans with individual cells inside. I looked out of the window and began to slightly regret my decision. It was like I was starting a life sentence, not 7 days on remand, but the sunshine and the sight of ordinary people going about their business made me worried. After all, I've never even visited a prison, let alone been sent to one.

Inside Durham prison we were strip searched and had to stand astride two benches naked whilst they shone a torch up my arse. It was totally humiliating. Then we were led inside into a reception area where we had to stand in front of a desk and be questioned individually. When my turn came I had perked up a bit and when I was asked my name I shouted 'Strike' in a defiant tone causing the warder to smirk. I gave my religion as 'Buddhist' in an attempt at humour and it made Keith Smoult laugh out loud. The warder wasn't amused and said, 'We'll soon put a stop to your piss taking, son.' That shut me up, even more when he asked my occupation and I said coal miner. He said, 'Ex-coal miner, son. You're Her Majesty's prisoner now'.

We were put into a room with a bench on each side. The walls were covered with rules and notices and as I was reading them my name was called and I was led into another room. Another warder came in and said I was being released and gave me back my belt and possessions and made me sign for them. I asked him what was going on but he just told me to stop moaning because there were hundreds of men inside who would love to be in my shoes.

I was then taken into an office where a woman handed me a bail form to sign. I refused and asked to see my lawyer. I asked why I was being released and she said she didn't know. I again refused and asked for a lawyer. She got angry then and said I could see one when I got out. I felt very guilty that I was letting the other lads down but I signed and was let out of the gate into brilliant sunshine with £1.64p, presumably my expenses. I walked up the hill to Red Hills, the Durham Area Headquarters and was shown into Jimmy Inskip's office. Jimmy is an ex-Westoe man and he got a shock and asked me if I'd escaped. I told him I had no idea why I'd been released. He rang the lawyers but he said they didn't know either but would investigate. He apologised for not being able to give me a lift but gave me £3 for my bus fare home.

Kath was very upset when I finally got home and says she feels like she is going to have a nervous breakdown with all the stress of work and worrying about me. I tried to reassure her and say the strike can't last for much longer. Trouble is, I don't believe it myself because there are no signs of it ending. What a fuckin' bastard of a day!!

Sunday June 10th, 1984

We travelled down to Doncaster for a meeting of miners who are either in the SWP or close to it. There were five of us from Westoe, Gary Marshall, Keith Smoult, me, and two younger lads, Ian Richardson and John Rumney, who we have been travelling to pickets with and selling the paper to. They are keen on politics but are confused about issues such as nuclear weapons and parliamentary democracy.

We arrived late due to a flat tyre but didn't miss too much. There were miners present from every coalfield except Wales, which is dominated by the Communist Party, and I was pleased to meet up with Ian Mitchell and Steve Hammill again. It was interesting to hear that I'm not the only one having problems with the union bureaucracy, and also that other areas were also having problems about raising the level of picketing. Steve Hammill spoke about the need to have mass pickets at Orgreave and also said that in his opinion Jack Taylor, President of Yorkshire Area, was deliberately preventing a mass picket by sending men into Notts where the policing was so high it was a complete waste of manpower. Another lad agreed and said we should picket NUM National HQ in Sheffield to draw attention to this. Steve said we shouldn't waste our time on union officials but organise the picketing ourselves at rank and file level. The most important target now is to picket steelworks such as Ravenscraig, Redcar, Scunthorpe and Llanwern. We need to go back to our pits and start arguing this case because it's the only way we can win. We need to really start fighting back against the Tories because everyone seems to be growing complacent. It was an excellent meeting and if it did nothing else it helped to make us all feel that we were not alone.

On the journey home we chatted to Ian and John about the issues we'd discussed and Gary was particularly convincing because he's finally joined the Party. Ian also told me that one of the committee men is spreading a rumour that the only reason I'd opted for jail was so that the forgery case against me would be dropped! Christ, those bastards are off their heads and just seem out to get me by any means. Why do I bother?

Keith also told me that the reason I got chucked out of prison was because I was charged with Obstruction of the Highway which isn't a prisonable offence. They were all charged with Obstruction of the Police, which is, and anyway they were all freed next day after lawyers appealed to a judge in chambers, whatever that means.

Tuesday June 12th, 1984

Today has been the most humiliating experience of my life!! I had been summonsed to appear in front of the whole Lodge Committee to explain my 'forgery' of the Lodge Secretary's signature. I was forced to wait outside of the committee room for twenty minutes, with my stomach churning and my nerves on edge wondering what was going to happen. When I was eventually called in I had to face them all whilst the Secretary again explained the seriousness of my action and how it couldn't be allowed to go unpunished. It was like a kangaroo court and in my opinion I was guilty before I entered. I explained exactly what I'd done and why I'd done it, pointing out that nowhere on the letter was either my name or address so there was no way I could make any kind of personal profit from it. I had only been trying to raise funds for the union.

My explanation fell on deaf ears and I was totally shocked when Tommy Wilson launched a personal attack of such a vicious nature I felt quite scared. He accused me of trying to overthrow the Lodge Committee and subvert the minds of the membership with my lunatic propaganda. He attacked the SWP and said I was their puppet, their 'agent of destruction'. It would have been laughable if it wasn't so serious. I was ordered to wait outside while they made their decision.

The bastards made me wait for another twenty minutes and it seemed like a lifetime as I thought about what they were going to do. It was terrible.

I was called back in and had to stand in front of them while sentence was pronounced. I am to appear in front of the whole Durham Executive on a charge of 'Fraudulent Conversion' which could result in my expulsion from the NUM! If Tommy Wilson has his way that's exactly what will happen. In addition I had to hand back the letter of authorisation and have been banned from ever collecting funds for the Lodge again. I was, and still am, stunned! Before I left I gave them a cheque for £120 I had received from Colin Barker in Manchester, made out to the Lodge, adding sarcastically that perhaps they didn't want any money I had collected. Tommy Wilson snarled that I should 'stuff it up my arse' but Slater was more diplomatic and thanked me, saying it was a shame I'd 'spoilt myself'.

I've made my decision to stuff the lot of them, union and SWP! Why should I stick my neck out? I'm going to stay at home and spend more time with Kath and the girls. I've done my bit and my reward has not been worth the fuckin' effort! I feel totally isolated and betrayed and it's not going to happen again. A couple of comrades have phoned and urged me to attend the union meeting tomorrow but I refused point blank. I can't face giving those bastards the satisfaction of reading out their decision to a packed hall. To be honest I feel too ashamed!

Wednesday June 13th, 1984

What a difference a day makes! I can hardly believe what has happened today and it has restored my faith in the strike and my fellow pickets. My phone has never stopped ringing this afternoon with my friends calling me to tell me what had happened, even though the Lodge Chairman had asked them not to because he wanted to ring me himself. He rang me at 5.15pm and I really enjoyed his discomfort as he informed me of the decision that had been made.

What happened was that Gary Marshall spoke to all the pickets in the new soup kitchen at Harton Miners Welfare when they returned from the morning picket. He told them that the food they were eating, and had been eating for weeks, had been paid for in part by money he and I had been collecting. He asked if anyone could cite a single case of dishonesty against me and then went out to give details of my personal commitment to the strike. He told them about what the Lodge Committee had done to me and finished by urging everyone to get down to the union meeting in the Armstrong Hall to speak in my defence. He said I was being witch hunted for being a member of the SWP.

The pickets all got into cars and left in convoy, stopping traffic and honking their horns and generally making a noise as they drove down Stanhope Road. They stormed into the Armstrong Hall and shocked the officials on the stage. When they found out the minutes had already been read they demanded they be read again. A vote was taken, won, and the minutes were re-read. When the minute concerning me was read out Gary jumped to his feet and proposed that all charges against me be dropped and this was quickly seconded but before a vote could be taken a heated debate developed with the end result being that the proposal was amended to say that I wouldn't have to appear in front of the Durham Executive but I was still banned from collecting funds and given a warning as to my future conduct. This was passed almost unanimously and caused visible displeasure to the platform. The bastards were seething! They were even more mad when a proposal was passed to give £3,000 to the Women's Support Group. The platform protested strongly but were easily defeated by the wishes of the majority. This was a great victory for the pickets because for the first time they could see that they made the decisions, the rank and file, and not the so called 'leaders' on the stage.

I felt so elated about what happened that I went along to our newly formed South Tyneside SWP branch meeting held in the North Eastern pub in South Shields this evening. We have split from Newcastle because that branch was becoming too big and people were able to hide from being actively involved. We are very optimistic about the future, especially Phil Turner, who only a few months ago was the only member in the town. Now there are five more members, all Westoe miners, and hopefully more will join.

The meeting was excellent because everyone was buzzing from today's events, especially Gary, and we all feel a lot more confident that SWP ideas really do work in practice.

Kath is pissed off again because I think she was looking forward to seeing more of me. However she is also relieved that the charges against me were dropped. A good day.

Thursday June 14th, 1984

This morning's picket at Woodside was quiet as usual but the pickets themselves were triumphant at what had happened yesterday and kept congratulating me. I had to tell them that I had done nothing and it was them who had done the hard work. I managed to sell 27 copies of *Socialist Worker* and pointed out Scargill's call to picket Orgreave. If we can force the Lodge to reverse decisions then we can also force them to send us to Orgreave.

Paul Foot has caused a real stir this week in the *Daily Mirror* by revealing documents that prove that Thatcher told British Rail bosses to make whatever concessions necessary to rail workers to stop a second front opening. I've been proudly telling pickets that Paul is an SWP member.

Friday June 15th, 1984

Today we attended a march and rally in Newcastle but it was very disappointing because Paul Foot missed a golden opportunity to support us.

We left the Armstrong Hall in two double decker buses provided by the TGWU and they were both full, not only with pickets but also the Women's Support Group and children. We assembled at Newcastle Civic Centre and the weather was gorgeous, hot and sunny and a large crowd was expected. There were Lodge banners from every pit in the North East plus lots of banners from other unions and political organisations. There were also hundreds of new placards from the SWP with the latest slogan, 'Turn Orgreave into Saltley' on one side, and 'Victory to the Miners' on the other. I was angry to see people ripping off the *Socialist Worker* bit at the top. Why do these people have to be so childish? The march was headed by the usual bunch of union bureaucrats and Labour MPs, with the mining Lodges behind and the rest behind us. The march was important because it showed the strength of our support to the ordinary people of Newcastle though I was disappointed that a strike had not been called at least for the day, with most unions only sending a token delegation. As we waited for the march to start I talked to a Nothumberland miner about the need to picket Orgreave and the steelworks. He surprised me by saying we shouldn't picket steelworks because we had no right to put the steel workers' jobs at risk. I explained that the steel workers had more chance of saving their jobs by supporting us because if we lost it was more than likely that the Tories would close at least one of the steelworks. I also pointed out that picketing Orgreave was vital because British steel had reneged on a deal to support the NUM and if we allowed them to get away with it the Tories would start to move coal stocks from pit yards because they would be confident. The lad seemed to agree with me and bought a copy of *Socialist Worker* and promised to argue the same with his mates on the picket line on Monday. This proves that arguments can be won if we take the trouble to have them.

The march set off and we got a great reception as we marched, with lasses from the WSG collecting with buckets. I was a bit disappointed with the turn out, which must have been about 10 to 15000, because we should have been able to attract at least double that number. Gary suggested we help the two women out who were struggling to carry their banner in the heat so we took over to give them a breather.

We entered Leazes Park on the Town Moor and looked for a place to sit. We were knackered and sat down gratefully. One of the pickets came over and told me he'd heard Tommy Wilson and his group discussing beating up anyone selling *Socialist Worker*. Just then Tommy and one of his lads turned up and asked Gary if they could have a word with him. Gary stood up warily and they moved a few yards away. I heard Wilson threatening to 'break' Gary's fuckin' legs for 'getting that commie bastard gonk Strike off the hook'. Wilson stormed off and Gary looked quite shaken, and who can blame him because Tommy is a hard bastard? We immediately gathered some other pickets and told them what had happened, prepared for a fight if we had to but still dreading it. Fortunately nothing else happened so we were relieved when Paul Foot was introduced on the stage.

He received a fantastic ovation from the crowd, especially from the miners because of his revelations about Thatcher and the rail workers. He spoke very well, calling for mass picketing at Orgreave and the need to stop steel. He attacked Kinnock for sitting on the fence and the NUM for having no centralised organisation to co-ordinate picketing activities. The only thing he didn't do was to say that he was himself a member of the SWP and that would have helped pickets like Gary and myself who are getting so much abuse for being in the Party and selling the paper. Like I said, he let us down. Anyway, he still got a tremendous round of applause and deserved it.

Mick McGahey followed, but was piss poor in comparison and was content to mouth slogans like 'No surrender'. Is that why he did a deal with Ravenscraig? He's living on his past record as a militant but he's now about as militant as Len Murray!

I did have the opportunity to mention my criticisms to Paul Foot in the pub afterwards but I didn't, probably because I didn't have the confidence in the face of his current popularity. I wish I had!

Tragically another picket was killed outside Ferrybridge power station today and that puts everything else that's happened today into second place by far. We can't give in now because two lads have given up their lives. Nothing is that important in comparison to a life lost!

Saturday June 16th, 1984

I did a paper sale in King Street, South Shields, and sold 37 papers. This has really given my confidence a boost and shows that there are people willing to listen to our ideas.

ORGREAVE

Sunday June 17th, 1984
Got a phone call this afternoon telling me that two coaches are leaving the Armstrong Hall at 3am tomorrow. My guess is they'll be going to Orgreave but no one knows for definite.

Kath is really pissed off and has warned me that I'd better slow down and pay more attention to her and the girls. She's right of course but I'm committed so what can I do?

Monday June 18th, 1984
I can honestly say I have never experienced anything like I did today and I hope I never do so again! It was terrifying and exciting at the same time and I've got the bruises and aching bones to prove it! Incredible.

I left home at 1.30am to walk the five miles from my house to the Armstrong Hall. It was quite pleasant for a change, warm and sultry, and I felt excited. I met up with Joe Humphries and Lol Calvert at the top of Stanhope Road and we talked on our way down. Lol said we were definitely going to Orgreave because he'd overheard two committee men talking last night. The Chairman, John Chapman, picked us up in his car and confirmed it was to be Orgreave and said he thought it was a waste of time and union funds. He also said Scargill should be negotiating with the NCB instead of calling for mass pickets because they only led to violence. I did mention Saltley Gate but it just flew over his head.

We all collected our £8 picket money and then piled aboard the two coaches. There were a few empty seats but I put that down to the early start because we set off dead on 3am. Most of the lads tried to catch a few hours kip but I was too excited and talked with Gary and Keith about what might happen. We thought it would be good to see some action after 14 weeks of almost no action and it could be just the kick up the arse the strike needed.

We arrived in Sheffield just after 6 after having been held up briefly by a convoy of coaches we thought were pickets, but saw they were actually pigs as we passed, hundreds of them, who turned off towards Orgreave. We had been told to meet outside of NUM HQ but when we got there we found the whole place in darkness and locked up. We were soon joined by 5 coaches full of Scottish pickets, and more pickets from Durham Lodges. No one seemed to know what to do until someone shouted through a megaphone and we all started to line up on the road to march to Orgreave because our coaches had already left to park up.

It must have been an amazing sight as hundreds of us headed for the motorway with Scots flags and banners at the head. The police had closed off the road and we marched along it chanting defiantly. It was a great feeling as there were surprisingly few pigs but we seemed to march for bloody miles. As we approached a slip road we saw it was lined with coaches. More pickets we thought until dozens of pigs began to pour out of them and came to march either side of our columns, trying to herd us into an organised mob. We responded by stopping then setting off again at different paces, the more energetic lads actually running, forcing the pigs to set off after them. Pretty soon we had strung ourselves out so much there were long sections totally unpoliced. This ended when we came to another slip road that was totally blocked off by pigs. I was glad because I was knackered and needed a rest. They kept us there for a good twenty minutes until even the slowest lads had caught up and then we found ourselves totally blocked in by pigs on all sides and prevented from leaving the march. Workers came out from factories to cheer us on and people caught in the traffic jam we'd probably caused honked their horns noisily in support. We were eventually filtered off to the left and found ourselves on a small country lane which petered out into a footpath, wide enough for only 3 abreast. There was a footbridge over a railway line and it was from the top of this that we caught our first sight of Orgreave.

There was the coke works in the distance, squatting on the land and belching out smoke from Yorkshire coal. A black line of police spread across the yellow field in front with horses to the rear and side. The pickets were to one side facing them and the whole scene was like a science fiction film, or a scene from the English Civil War! As I reached the bottom of the footbridge I heard lots of shouting and noise in the distance and guessed it was a clash between police and pickets so I and everyone else began to run up the lane. After a few hundred yards we could see hundreds of pickets running up the field with pigs on horses in hot pursuit. It was an awesome sight and I remember thinking that there were more pickets than horses and they could easily beat them. It was only later when I was in the mass picket that I found out for myself the panic that spreads instantly when the horses charge and makes you react without thinking!

We joined the pickets at the top of the field as the horses were returning behind police lines and I spotted a lad I'd met at Skegness whose name is Dermot and he filled me in about what had happened. The cavalry charge had been in response to a few nutters throwing bricks from the back of the picket. Dermot had been hit twice by a baton and had two very painful lumps, one on his side and one on his shoulder. It hadn't stopped him from trying to sell *Socialist Worker*, which is how he'd ended up in the frontline in the first place because some pickets had given him the usual abuse about being more interested in selling the paper than in fighting the pigs, so he went to the front to show them they were wrong. We talked for a while and tried to guess the size of the picket, coming to the conclusion that there were more of us than them, but we felt that there still weren't enough pickets to really make a difference. The police stretched across the field dressed in full riot gear, standing behind huge plastic shields, with mounted police also in riot gear behind them. It was a chilling sight, especially as we faced them dressed only in t-shirts and jeans. How could we beat them? The answer was, of course, mass pushes, but we reckoned there were only about 5,000 of us whilst at the famous victory at Saltley Gate in 1972 there had been 15,000, and the miners then had been reinforced by other workers. The SWP had produced placards saying 'Turn Orgreave into Saltley' but it didn't look like we had enough to make it a reality. Scargill was with us, but where were McGahey, Heathfield, Taylor and the rest?

Dermot and me made our way down to the front and I scanned the pickets looking for familiar faces. I saw Tommy Wilson and his sons just in front of me, and when Tommy spotted me he came over and said, 'We've had our differences in the past, Strike, but at least you've got the guts to be where the action will be and I respect you for that. Not like those jelly backed bastards back there,' he snarled, pointing at the vast majority of pickets who were as far back up the road as they could get, with hundreds more standing on walls that lined the road. Suddenly a hail of missiles began to fly over our heads and land amongst the police line. We all shouted at them to stop and come down the front with us if they wanted to throw stuff. A lad near me went down screaming, felled by a lump of stone with blood oozing from the back of his head. As lads went to help him and get him to his feet the police line parted and without warning the horses charged out closely followed by pigs in riot gear with round shields. I just ran to the side of the road and jumped down the embankment, thinking I would be safer there. Dozens of others did the same but to our shock the pigs came after us, and not only that, hidden to our right were police with dogs which they began to unleash. That was all I needed for the adrenalin to kick in and I began sprinting up the field trying to avoid the slower lads. I made it to safety but was horrified at what I saw as I looked back down the field. Dogs were biting lads whilst others were being truncheoned by pigs and either led away or dragged away! It was a disgusting sight and one I never ever thought I'd see in this country. I'll never forget it but even worse was to follow.

Back on the road Arthur Scargill was standing, wearing a baseball hat and shouting through a megaphone saying, 'Come on lads! Don't run from a few mounted police. I've seen bigger horses at York races. Get down the front for a push. There's enough of us to break them'! Some of the lads started off down the road but the majority just stayed where they were taking no notice. Scargill then shouted, 'I'm ashamed to see miners standing by while their comrades are fighting for their jobs!' Even this didn't shift the cowardly bastards and as I made my way back down to the front I could hear him still pleading for more men to join us. I lit up a cigarette which was a mistake because I didn't even have time to take a drag before we started to move forward and crashed into the police line and my arm was trapped by the crush. We managed to force them back a few yards before their line was reinforced and they pushed us back. An angry picket shouted at me to get rid of the cigarette and I managed to drop it, burning a hole in my t shirt as I did so. I struggled to keep my feet in the crush as we were being forced back. The shout went up of 'Man down' and this ended the push as it always did. The pigs seized the chance to grab anyone they could and I saw a few bodies disappear behind police lines. This angered some of the pickets and I saw one lad launch himself feet first at the police whilst another small group managed to wrestle free a riot shield which they waved defiantly at the pigs. I also saw one of our 'Turn Orgreave into Saltley' placards being held aloft by a picket standing right in front of the pigs. He was a lot braver than me.

I decided to move into the field on my right, determined not to get stuck in the middle of another push. The feeling of claustrophobia always frightens me in a push, the feeling that you're about to faint because of the pressure crushing you ribs and making breathing difficult. I hate it yet always seem to forget and find myself in another push despite my avowals of never again. I spotted Dave Hayes, who used to live in Newcastle but now lived in Sheffield and who I'd met at the Skegness weekend. He was talking to a woman who was introduced to me as Sheila McGregor (a worse surname than mine!). It was a glorious hot day with heatwaves shimmering in front of the police line making them look even more unreal than they were. The three of us stood talking about what needed to be done, and I took off my shirt and tied it round my waist, enjoying the heat of the sun on my back. Some lads had set fire to the captured riot shield and the stubble in the field had caught fire. We were trying to stamp it out when Sheila told me my trousers were on fire. They laughed as I jumped about trying to put the smouldering jeans out. The police must have been wound up because I just had time to see the police line part and the horses move forward before turning tail and starting to sprint up the field to avoid being caught. Believe me, running up a field in steel toe capped boots in scorching heat is not to be recommended, but the sound of galloping hooves and the occasional whoosh of a baton being aimed at your head is a wonderful incentive to breaking the pain barrier, and probably the world record for the 400m! I sped past other lads running and reached a wall at the top of the field and dove over the top, heedless of what might lie beyond. I went tumbling down a steep railway embankment and landed painfully at the bottom at the side of a railway line. I dusted myself off and began to gingerly climb back up, watching for police as I climbed. As I watched I saw the horses returning behind the lines whilst all over the field there were riot police beating miners while others were being dragged away. I could see one pig repeatedly clubbing a lad as he lay helpless on the ground. Any respect that I may have had for the police disappeared today. I've seen riots on TV, Brixton, Toxteth etc but this was different because it was my fellow miners being clubbed for nothing more than fighting for the right to work. If this is how Thatcher intends defeating us then I for one will never give in!

We eventually made our way back down the field but I met Gary Marshall and he told me that our coaches were going and we had to leave. I couldn't believe it! We couldn't leave now and desert the battle. We made our way back up the field and met Tommy Wilson. He had been badly clubbed when he was trying to help an injured picket and was in a lot of pain. I advised him to get to hospital to have his injuries looked at. We reached the bridge and found most of our lads talking with Scargill. They had told him about us being ordered to leave and Arthur was furious and told us to stay and fight back. He complained bitterly about the waste of union funds in just sending us down for the day instead of for the whole week. He also said that if necessary he would pay for our transport himself. We all voted to stay because none of us wanted to leave anyway, not without having another go at the pigs. We wanted revenge.

We were all starving, so when we saw lads passing with bags of food and drink we decided to go in search of the shop, which must be nearby. A few hundred yards up the road we found hundreds of lads sitting and lying outside of a supermarket, a lot of them drinking beer and cider, and getting pissed by the look of them. One criticism I would make of the union is probably not shared by most miners, but I'll say it anyway. £8 a day 'subsistence allowance' was too much, and £4 would be enough, especially for a one day visit. A lot of lads took money home for their families but a lot also seemed to abuse it and get pissed, which does nothing to enhance a mass picket and leaves us open to criticism from the media.

Anyway, Gary, Keith and I went into the supermarket where I bought some bread rolls, cheese and a carton of milk, and Keith spent ages deciding what to have but ended up getting crisps. We went back outside and found a seat on the wall and settled down to eat hungrily. I noticed a couple of lads looking hungrily at us and I offered them some bread and cheese. It turned out they were striking miners from Nottingham and they had only been given petrol money because their union funds were frozen. I gave them £2 and Gary and Keith did the same. They were embarrassingly grateful but we told them that we were grateful for them striking when they were in the minority, and we discussed how hard life was for them. One of them gave me his union badge and I was really touched. We left to rejoin the picket feeling really humble.

When we got to the bridge we found that the pigs had taken advantage of the pickets' absence and moved their line right up and refused to let anyone pass. This caused a lot of anger and as more pickets returned the anger turned into action and we all started to throw anything we could grab at the pigs and forced them to retreat under a hail of missiles. I spotted Ian Mitchell, a comrade from Silverwood Colliery, and we both criticised the pigs for preventing us returning to picket and causing the violent response. It wasn't helping our cause but there was nothing could be done to stop it.

The pigs regrouped and charged forward wielding their batons and everyone just turned tail and ran. I cursed the slower men in front of me as I stumbled forward and was relieved when we came to a halt a few hundred yards up the road because the police had retreated again. The word buzzed around that Scargill had been injured and arrested in the charge and this only infuriated the pickets further and gave them a fresh incentive to attack the pigs. At the bridge a group of pickets were dragging a car across the road from a repair yard to the right of the bridge. I joined in, by now so infuriated that I was prepared to do anything to stop the pigs charging again. The car burst into flames, set alight by an unknown hand, and everyone cheered and taunted the pigs who were unable to get us because of the burning car and the constant hail of missiles being thrown at them. Local residents started to put bottles of water out on their garden walls and these were eagerly taken by us, grateful for the water in the scorching heat. It was good to see they seemed to be on our side.

Something had to happen because the pigs could not afford to be beaten, and sure enough the horses returned through the black smoke causing wild panic and pickets were running in all directions to get away. I'll never forget the fear I felt as a horse just missed trampling me and fortunately the pig was busy trying to club someone else so I got away. I saw a man run up a metal staircase and the bloody horse was trying to follow him! It was incredible. I ran to where I thought safety lay with the majority of the lads in front of the supermarket but the pigs had scented blood and were hell bent on getting at us, charging forward into the crowd. I was off and running again ran into the supermarket car park and hid behind some cars. The noise of shouting and pain was everywhere. I crept over to join some other pickets hiding behind a car nearby. They were Welsh, and were older men, unlike the majority of us. One of them looked like he was having a heart attack as he gasped for breath, his face contorted with pain. His two mates didn't look much better but after a while they seemed better. One of them told me that when the police had charged they were at the back but were caught unawares and had only avoided capture by running into the supermarket. Security guards had chased them out and they had to run to where they were now.

After about ten minutes I decided to venture back onto the main road, leaving the Welsh lads behind because they said they would take no risks. There was no sign of the police and a large crowd stood on the road. A group of drunk Scots chanted, 'We're mental, we're crazy, we're off wor fuckin' heeds' and aimed kicks at any vehicle that went past. I went into the supermarket to ring Kath and tell her I was ok. She told me that Orgreave was all over the news and that the miners had been violent. That made me laugh but I told her I'd explain when I got home, probably about nine.

The Westoe lads were called together because our coaches had arrived. Some lads had gone into Sheffield to get them and we couldn't now see any reason to stay because it had all gone crazy and it would be pointless having lads arrested. A head count was taken and men sent out to round up stragglers. There was a rumour going round that the police would arrest anyone still left, just like in Mansfield. We boarded our coach for safety and waited until the lads sent out returned, then set off to Sheffield to pick up some of our lads who had been taken to hospital. One of them, Fred Taylor, told us how he'd been beaten in the first push. He's a big lad and has a plastic hip so he couldn't run like the rest of us and he just stood as a pig ran up and clubbed him to the ground and then beat him about the ribs. He was lucky not to have been arrested. None of our lads had been arrested but a few had been injured. A lot of others weren't so fortunate and it's a bloody miracle no one was murdered!

The journey home was very quiet, with most of us catching up on our sleep. We weren't depressed, more angry at what we'd seen, and most of us would have stayed the week if someone had arranged it. One thing we were all clear about is that we will not give in and the more the state throws against us the more determined we are to fight back.

Kath and me watched scenes on the news tonight but the slant they put on it made us seem like the aggressors. They showed none of the bad things they did against us. Looks like we're on our own.

POLICE & THIEVES

Monday June 25th, 1984
Since the disaster at Orgreave I've spent my time at Woodside Drift Mine. The best thing that can be said about it is that at least we kept a van load of pigs away from Tow Law. It has given me the chance to build a good relationship with other pickets and sell *Socialist Worker* plus discussing the strike. We also play football but I ruined my shoes and have had to buy another pair for £4.99. No more football!

After picketing we had a dinner of fishcake and chips in the soup kitchen and it was there I learned that I am one of 16 men pulled from a hat to go on flying picket duty. The fact that over 100 men wanted to go has caused a lot of resentment amongst the lads not chosen, especially those who've been active since day one. I can't see why the Lodge can't send all the men who want to go because they are risking men just giving up and staying at home.

I was told to report to the hall for 6pm so I went home and flung some clothes into a bag, slung a sleeping bag over my shoulder and then caught a bus down to Kath's workplace. We had a coffee together whilst I buttered her up before telling her I was off again for a few days on a flying picket. She accepted this with a resigned look on her face and was not upset as I'd expected her to be. She must be getting used to it. We walked into town at 5pm and parted at the bus stop with a kiss.

At the hall I signed for my £32 and was told we'd probably be home for Thursday. The only thing that Slater would tell us was that we were heading for Scotland so it was likely we would be going to Bilston Glen where they have scabs and also where a lot of Durham lads have already been arrested.

Typically we had to wait two hours for the coach to arrive and because we'd been paid a lot of the lads took the opportunity to have a pint or five which made for a boisterous journey. As for the Manchester trip last month there were four pits represented: Sacriston, Herrington, Wearmouth and us. The driver took a discrete route over the border because we didn't want to be stopped by the pigs, and we had to make quite a few piss stops so we didn't get to Dalkeith Miners Welfare until after midnight.

So here we are, lying on the seats in the concert room after being fed a supper of soup and bread. The possibility of sleep is looking remote seeing as a pool competition is taking place (it's 2.24am!). We've been told that picketing starts at 5am but have been promised better accommodation later today. I bloody hope so because I am shattered.

Tuesday June 26th, 1984

I got no sleep at all last night, and after picketing at Bilston Glen this morning I managed to grab an hour in the TV room of the club before being turfed out by the cleaning woman.

Scotland's showpiece pit didn't impress by its outward appearance, looking tiny in comparison with Westoe and Wearmouth. We all assembled at a social club just down the road from the pit and a man who the Scots lads called 'Gaddafi' made it perfectly clear that he was in charge and would organise tactics.

We followed him up the road until we were forced to halt by a double line of police across the road. Gaddafi urged us to follow him, about 200 of us, and we made our way through a housing estate and ended up on a road that ran at right angles to the pit. Apparently 'scabs' drove up this road and we were going to stop them by blocking it off. We lined up across the road and initially caught the police napping but not enough men were prepared to attack the pit entrance and the police arrived in numbers and also lined up across the road so were facing each other. Within minutes a push began and we forced them back a few yards before police started rushing in from behind us and a lot of men scattered. We fell back and regrouped, linked arms and clashed heavily with the pigs, forcing them slowly backwards until the cry of 'Man down!' went up and forced us to ease off, only to discover no one was down and we'd been conned by the pigs. The pigs took full advantage of our confusion and began forcing us backwards, with some of the bastards lashing out viciously with feet and fists. Some of us retaliated and a few lads were lifted and dragged away through police lines.

There was a building site to our right and some of the lads grabbed bricks from here and began throwing them at the advancing pigs. This caused the pigs to draw their truncheons and charge at us. We beat a hasty retreat and I was one of those fortunate enough to get away unscathed and I cautiously made my way back to the main entrance where the rest of the picket was spent without any further incident.

As we were about to leave at 8.30 I spotted the Scots NUM leaders, Mick McGahey and Eric Clarke, coming through police lines. They joined the 'official' six man picket. I asked them if it was possible to co-ordinate the pickets more effectively so we could concentrate our forces at the best points. McGahey's reply is classic: 'Picketing has nothing to do with me, son.' I should have known better than to ask such a question of such a leading fighter in the class war!

We had breakfast in Dalkeith before being told to gather our things together for a move to better accommodation. Gary and I were to stay with a lad called Kenny McCormack, whom we'd met at the SWP miners' meeting in Doncaster. We were going to stay at his uncle's house in Arniston, a small mining village about 7 miles from Edinburgh. We put our stuff in the house and then had dinner in the local Miners Welfare, soup followed by mince and 'tatties'. I just had the soup and 'tatties' because I'm a vegetarian, much to the amusement of my fellow pickets. We'd barely time to breathe before we set off for the afternoon picket at Bilston Glen.

The sun was burning hot and I was dressed for it in white jacket, white shirt, trousers and white shoes. The lads all took the piss and voted me best dressed picket but I was going to the theatre after the picket and wanted to look smart as I could.

There was an excellent turn out of about 400 men and at least 50 women and we were all confident of a breakthrough. We all linked arms and formed up into a solid block on the road, marching towards the police lines chanting, 'Here we go, here we go!'

The pigs didn't know what hit them as we forced them back strongly. Unfortunately double decker buses full of pigs began to arrive to reinforce their lines and stopped our progress. The crush was terrible and I lost my shoe, having difficulty hopping on one leg to avoid my foot from being trampled. The push broke down as the pigs started hitting lads again and we scattered. I went back to find my shoe and was lucky to get it. One of my Westoe mates wasn't so lucky and got arrested whilst doing the same thing, and two of his mates, Bede and Gordon, were lifted with him. It was a bad day for arrests, with over 30 lads lifted, but that has just made us more determined to return in the morning for another go.

I made my way into Edinburgh to watch my mate, Stuart Hepburn, perform in Chekhov's *Three Sisters*. I did feel a bit out of place amongst all the posh perfume and people but I really enjoyed the play. It was excellent, and it was nice to catch up with Stuart afterwards and have a few pints. He kindly paid for a taxi back to Arniston but I couldn't remember Kenny's address and so was forced to find our coach, and I'll have to kip here tonight.

Wednesday June 27th, 1984
I was roused from my sleep at 4.30am by the first of the lads arriving for picket duty. Gary took me to Kenny's house and I quickly changed into more suitable clothes before rushing back to the coach. One of the Scots lads told us that we were to be used as decoys to divert police, whilst the

main body of pickets made a concerted push at the main gate.

Accordingly we were forced to stand at a windy junction for two hours and achieved absolutely nothing except frustrating ourselves. We should have been with the main body of pickets trying to build on yesterday's success but the best I could do was voice this opinion loudly and criticise the Scots leaders for poor organisation. Most of our lads agreed with me, so at least that's something.

The afternoon was spent at an open cast site called Bonnyrigg and at least here we had some small success in managing to turn back two lorries purely by putting our case to the drivers. This proves that peaceful picketing does work if the pigs are not there to provoke confrontation. The lads all noticed this and we all felt really confident.

Thursday June 28th, 1984

After the early morning picket at Bilston Glen, which was without incident, or any pushes, we set off for the journey home. Our visit was not an entire waste of time because at least the number of scabs hasn't gone up as the NCB were hoping for, and we've all gained some valuable experience. We need real mass pickets to really make a difference to this strike and that means trying to get the majority of men who are sitting on their arses at home out onto the picket lines. More importantly we need to make sure we aim our pickets at the right targets and just now that means steelworks.

Anyway, it's nice to be back home with the family.

Friday June 29th, 1984

It was back to reality this morning with the usual picket at Woodside. It really is a waste of time going there because we never ever see anyone going in or out. Its only value is to talk with the other pickets and try to agitate for our Lodge officials to up the activity and send more men to places like Bilston Glen.

I got a phone call from Maureen Watson at *Socialist Worker* and she has asked me if I would write a review of *Germinal* by Emile Zola for the paper. I said I'd love to because it's one of my favourite novels and I must be one of the few people who actually read it down a coal mine when I was studying for an Open University course last year.

I spent the rest of today going back over it and I'm amazed by the similarities between the main character, Etienne, and Scargill. At least it will provide a bit of diversion from the boredom of Woodside.

Saturday June 30th, 1984

This morning saw the 'Coal Not Dole' march and rally organised by our Lodge officials. It was a very disappointing turn out, only a few thousand people, but it could have been so much better if they'd told us about it and allowed us, the rank and file, to have some part in the organisation. All the Durham Lodges were represented, plus a couple from Yorkshire and Kent, but when you consider the coal mining traditions of South Shields, which once boasted 3 pits, with even more in the close vicinity, then it was disappointing. I suppose that because the town has lost most of its industries and has a high level of unemployment, apathy is part of life.

We marched from the Armstrong Hall to the Bents Park on the seafront, and if anything, the rally was even more of a disappointment than the march. The speakers were abysmal. Our Lodge Secretary introduced Jack Taylor of Yorkshire Area NUM as 'a future legend of the trade union movement'. Leg end is more like it! It was him who signed the deal to allow coal into Scunthorpe steelworks, allowing them to break productivity records! He was full of empty rhetoric and received only lukewarm applause. Jim Slater was applauded only because of the seamen's support, and because he's from Shields, as his speech was boring, and only Jack Collins of Kent NUM came out with any credibility.

Its typical of the total lack of organisation at Westoe that we couldn't even hold a decent rally. Pathetic.

Friday July 6th — Monday July 9th, 1984

Keith Smoult, Gary Marshall and myself travelled down to London to attend 'Marxism 84' at the University of London.

Keith and myself, along with Yunus Bakhsh were allocated lodgings with a lovely Irish woman called Anne in Holloway (not the prison!). She made us feel very welcome and didn't complain if we came back late, which we mostly did. Also, we were usually pissed because comrades kept buying us beer. It was a really welcome break from the boredom of Woodside, and I for one learnt a lot.

We attended as many meetings as we could, eager to meet new people and learn about loads of things we knew nothing about. The highlights for me were Paul Foot on 'From Wilson to Kinnock, the Tragedy and the Farce', Chris Bambery on 'Ireland', Duncan Hallas on 'The French Revolution', Ian Birchall on 'Emile Zola' (brilliant!), and Tony Cliff on everything!!

Socially it was excellent and it was great to meet up with Ian Mitchell and Steve Hammill again. We had a miners' fringe meeting where we discussed our fears of a sell out of the strike because of the 'constructive talks' taking place between MacGregor and the NUM, and the vapid outpourings of Heathfield, Taylor, McGahey and co. Steve Hammill has drawn up a leaflet that outlines what constitutes a sell out, and what a victory should be, including the divisive Incentive Scheme being scrapped and the average integrated into our basic rate of pay, a minimum 15% pay rise, reinstatement of all sacked miners, retirement at 55, a 4 day week, and no pit closures without consultation. It was just heartening to talk with lads in the same situation as ourselves about positive things instead of the apathy we have to face on a daily basis. We should get together more often!

Keith and me were so broke over the weekend that we had to walk back to Holloway after meetings, and on Sunday had to share a plate of chips between us for dinner. Sheila McGregor noticed, bless her, and gave us £5 each. We celebrated with a takeaway meal and caught the tube back to Holloway instead of walking.

We had to come home on Monday, partly because I am up in court on Wednesday, but also to appease our wives. That's one thing the three of us do share in common, and it isn't getting any better as the strike drags on!

FIGHTING THATCHER

Wednesday July 11th, 1984
I finally appeared in court in Bishop Auckland to face the heinous charge of 'Obstruction of the Highway' after being arrested at the start of May. This has been one of the tactics the Tories have used to prevent us from being effective, and it bloody worked. Bastards! I tried to defend myself but to no avail and was found guilty and fined the maximum £50, with £30 costs, to be paid back at £1 a week due to my having no income. No real complaints because the pigs only lied a little bit. At least I don't have to go back to Woodside and can resume picketing at Tow Law so it was well worth it!

Saturday July 14th, 1984
Today should have been the 101st Durham Miners Gala but because of the strike it's been called a rally instead. I fail to see the logic behind the name change but there you go.

The Westoe contingent, two bus loads, left the Armstrong Hall at 8.45, half an hour late due to yet another cock up by our Lodge officials. It was pissing done with rain, and on a normal Gala day this wouldn't have dampened our spirits but 18 weeks into a strike it did. Everyone seemed quiet, though a few of the pickets were in a very optimistic mood due to the dockers having come out on strike earlier this week and they talked enthusiastically about Thatcher not being able to fight on two fronts. Admittedly the dockers have the power to really damage the Tories but the bastards are clever and I can't see them letting it happen. They've come too far and will find a way to compromise, just as they did with the railway workers. I hope I'm wrong, but the TV and papers are doing all they can to stop a dual front.

The rain was still pouring down when we arrived in Durham and we tramped onto a wet field to get ready for the march. I had brought Jennifer and Sasha along with me and they were just enjoying the whole experience. Kath had refused to come, choosing to go shopping instead. I wasn't too surprised when it was discovered that the poles for our lodge banner had gone missing, and when they were finally found and fitted, we were almost last in the procession.

There were banners from every coalfield, including Scotland and Wales, and it was a really colourful spectacle. We lined up behind the Cortonwood banner and there were 'Victory to the Miners' and 'Unite to Fight' placards everywhere. Some people had even turned some of them into rain hats. The brass bands were playing and we set off to march through the city, down towards the racecourse by the river where the rally was to be held. Jennifer and Sasha's faces were glowing with pride as crowds of people lined the streets and cheered us on, and I was proud as well, proud to be fighting back against Thatcher and the Tories.

Scargill gave his usual defiant speech, full of passion and anger at those unions not supporting us. Dennis Skinner was excellent, equally full of passion and fire, and one of the true Socialists in the Labour Party. A low point for me was Betty Heathfield, wife of Peter, General Secretary of the NUM, who was appealing for Women's Support Groups to come down to London so they could hand a petition to that champion of the working classes, the Queen! I hope no one turns up!

The real moment of magic came when Kneel Kinnock stepped up to the microphone and made most of the crowd disappear, but not before they'd booed him loudly for his traitorous lack of support for miners and their families. The bastard is more concerned about getting Labour elected than he is about his core supporters, and he even had the nerve to criticise violence on the picket lines. I was glad to see people turn their back on him and walk away, especially as this was the same man who only a year ago had got a standing ovation. Miners at least now see him for the soft reformist he is.

Anyway, despite the rain it was a good day out and the girls enjoyed playing with other kids whose dads were also on strike. I'm glad I took them.

Monday July 23rd, 1984

I had an early start to the day, getting up at 3.30am so I could get to the Armstrong Hall for 4.30 and get a lift to Tow Law. My first day back since May and it was a big disappointment. Apathy was rampant and there were only about 100 pickets. Just a bit of loud shouting when the lorries sped in. The 'highlight' of the picket was when someone threw an egg at a copper and missed by a mile.

The order came through to call in at the Philadelphia Workshops near Houghton le Spring where there was a picket to try and stop COSA staff from going into work. I had a run in with a vicious pig who really pushed me hard in the chest for no reason other than I was facing him! I went for him but some lads came to my rescue and we got away from the front. Time to go home.

This afternoon I got a phone call from Gary telling me that a coach was leaving from the hall to go to Scotland and that 55 men were required. I rang the union and volunteered and was told to report to the hall with a sleeping bag at 5.30pm.

I went down to the Women's Aid Refuge and told Kath I was off to Scotland again. She seemed resigned and warned me not to get arrested. She told me to be careful and ring to let her know what was going on.

We arrived at Dalkeith Strike Centre at 9.30pm and it was a much more relaxed journey than the one we had last month. We only stayed a few minutes whilst details of accommodation were picked up. We were to be in Arniston and Penicuik but a bit of a row broke out because the people in Arniston wanted the people who stayed there last week to return. This caused the lads who hadn't stayed there to think it was the best place to stay and demanded that the 'rubs be put in'. I couldn't be arsed to join in such a petty squabble so I volunteered for Penicuik. The SWP already has a few members there so I wanted to experience something new, and meet more people.

After dropping off half the men in Arniston we headed for Penicuik, stopping off at Shottstown Miners Welfare for a piss. I was not too surprised to see the two union officials from Westoe, sent to help co-ordination, were with us, leaving no one in Arniston to co-ordinate with. We spotted none other than Mick McGahey sitting at a table full of empty whisky glasses. A lot of the lads were excited to see him but not me. I'd met him before, and also heard loads of tales.

We were given soup and bread, and a free pint, and as were eating Mick came swaying over to give us a pep talk. His speech was slurred and it was sad to see a man who was once one of the top fighters in the NUM reduced to a drunken old man. He spoke of his hope of renewed talks bringing about a quick settlement, but when men started to ask questions about the Incentive Scheme, the 4 day week, sacked miners he just put on his most sincere face and voice and promised us there'd be no sell out! He put enough money behind the bar for 2 pints for each man so we all cheered loudly as he left. He called back and said he was seeing Arthur in the morning and he would tell him what a fine body of men we are. Bullshit!

Exit Mick Senior, enter Mick Junior, a big lad with thick glasses, curly hair and a flair for organisation. Within minutes we had all been allocated places to stay and were on our way.

Dave Butchard, Micky Cunningham, Andy Halliday and me were all sent to the home of Willie and Marlene Forsyth. Andy got the couch because he's ancient, over 50, Keith, Micky and me got the son's bedroom, a bit cramped but fine. As I try to note this down 'Butch' is poncing round the floor in his silk underpants, a horrible sight, and I get a strong feeling we won't get much sleep because Butch is mad as a hatter. Anyway, the Forsyths have made us feel really at home so roll on tomorrow.

Tuesday July 24th, 1984

We didn't get much sleep but Butch is so likeable that you can't get mad at him. We had a breakfast off hot egg rolls and coffee which set us up nicely for the morning, and we waited outside for the bus to Bilston Glen.

The first person I met was John Sturrock, who is a photographer, an excellent one, but we barely had time to talk before the first push began and I joined the front rank, linking arms with the pickets either side of me. The initial clash was a violent one, with the front rank of the pigs kicking hell out of us whilst the rank behind tried to punch us. At one point the lines seemed to reverse, with us pushing the opposite way, but it was bloody chaotic, and very painful. My shins were actually bleeding and the whole experience was intensely claustrophobic and the push eventually broke down. We could see lads had been arrested and being dragged away, whilst two men were being carried into ambulances on stretchers! We angrily regrouped and charged into the pigs, but their lines had been reinforced by busloads of pigs. The push was broken up by some idiot throwing a rotten goose egg, and the resulting stench actually saw a few lads throwing up. We made a half hearted third attempt but were too weak and it soon broke up with a few more arrests. We had to content ourselves with shouting abuse at the handful of scabs who went in.

The afternoon was a huge disappointment after the excitement of the morning because we didn't have enough pickets and there was no attempt to organise, with the majority enjoying the hot sunshine.

We went to the local Miners Welfare this evening and most of the lads got pissed, including Butch, so hopefully that means we can sleep tonight.

Wednesday July 25th, 1984

The mood of the men this morning was very militant, especially amongst the Durham lads, and I saw all the lads I've come to respect, Tommy Ashurst from Easington, and 'Cosh' from Herrington, and lads from Wearmouth and Sacriston, all of them up for a fight.

This morning's picket began with a push that was quickly broken up by cowardly bastards throwing stones from the back, one of them hitting a lad just in front of me and splitting the back of his head open. Some of us ran to the back of the picket and told the lads either join the push or fuck off!! We formed up again and linked arms, but this time I was on the outside of the front line, I was trying to avoid the crush for once but there wasn't much difference. We crashed into the police lines and began a strong push. The 'Man down' shout went up but this time most of us ignored it and continued pushing. As I was out on the edge I could move more and to my shock I spotted a man getting trampled on the floor. I shouted for help and grabbed his arm and began pulling him out. Other lads helped and we got him to the side of the road. He looked in his fifties and his face was white and he was unconscious. Another lad took over who said he was a first aider and I rejoined the push. It broke up angrily, and the pickets were furious because there'd been loads of arrests and at least a dozen lads injured. The man I helped pull out had had a heart attack but was still alive as they took him away. The lads were saying that the pigs had been vicious and had deliberately tripped lads up and then gave them a kicking when they were down! Punches were aimed at stomachs and faces and the violence had really gone up from the pigs.

Our response was a hail of missiles raining down on the pigs, with loud cheers when one went down. In my opinion that was just stupid because it'll just make them worse next time we clash. Anyway the situation was defused by one of the Scottish union officials telling everyone to assemble at the Dalkeith Strike Centre for a special meeting to discuss tactics. A real novelty.

When our coach got there we were given a standing ovation from the Scots pickets for our support, and the 100 Durham lads already arrested and in hospital. There must have been about 700 men in the hall and I was wondering how we could never get more than 200 on the picket line.

The Delegate from Monktonhall gave a rip roaring speech that spoke of defying the police and ended by urging us all to go to Bilston Glen 'the noo', and take the pigs by surprise and take control of the main entrance to the pit. This was greeted with loud roars of approval and we all started to pile out of the hall and into cars and coaches to take the 'Glen'. There was a real positive buzz on our coach because we felt there was a real chance of us achieving something solid. We were wrong!

Our coach was the first to arrive and we filed out and stood defiantly in front of the gate, which was 'guarded' by a few security men. More lads started to arrive in dribs and drabs but not the hundreds we were expecting. At most we were 200 but at least our hosts from Arniston and Penicuik stood alongside us. Some of us wanted to invade the pit and occupy it because our numbers were too small to hold the gate. Lads started to talk about riot police with dogs being inside the pit so we just stood in front of the entrance with the sun beating down on us. The only event of any note was the arrival of a car full of pensioners come to see about their fuel allowance so we let them through. The guards turned them back and I guessed that meant we were in for trouble.

I had just taken off my shirt and given it to Marlene, who was across the road, for safe keeping when double decker buses full of pigs started to arrive. I ran back and joined the back row of pickets right in front of the barrier and gasped. There were bloody hundreds of them, lining up in ranks and marching to stand in front of us. There were ambulances and police vans rolling up, and they started to rush into the pit yard behind us, coming from the sides. We linked arms and steeled ourselves.

We didn't stand a chance! We were bloody massacred! Without any warning they crashed into our front ranks and forced us back. I was terrified that I was going to break my back as we were forced hard up against the barrier so I pushed forward with all my might to get away. Suddenly an arm snaked around my neck and I was choking and forced to leave go of the lads on either side of me as I struggled to free the arm. I kicked backwards and the arm went and I pushed forward again. My luck ran out when my arm was grabbed and in an instant I found myself up against the barrier facing two pigs. One of them grabbed me by my ears and pulled me over the barrier and I landed on my head. I felt blood on my face but before I could do anything boots started to fly into me and I tried to curl up to protect myself, arms covering my face. I'll never forget one of the pigs saying as he kicked, 'Ah'll teach you to interrupt ma fuckin' dinner.' It would have been funny if it hadn't been so bloody painful. They dragged me over to a van and literally threw me into the back of it, where I was badly trampled by some pigs getting out. One bastard deliberately kicked me in the head as he got out! A picket helped me onto the bench that lined the van and I was suffering from double vision and pain everywhere. Another man was thrown into the van and even with my blurred vision I could see he was in trouble with his breathing and was in a lot of pain. A lad shouted for an ambulance but they just ignored us. The man was also helped onto the bench.

After a hazy 10 minutes or so in the van I was roughly grabbed and told to get out, then I was frogmarched to another van with my arm up my back and shoved in. The first thing I saw was Butch grinning at me and I sat next to him. We swapped tales of how we'd been lifted whilst a poor lad lay on the floor with a broken ankle moaning loudly. He was in agony and his face was contorted with pain. The whole thing was made worse because it was sweltering hot inside the van because we had no ventilation. We shouted for an ambulance and the door opened and a pig told us one had been sent for. We could plainly see an ambulance just outside and when we pointed this out the pig told us it was for police use only! I couldn't believe it and said to Butch that they wouldn't be putting that on the telly or in the papers. That lad was forced to wait for 35 minutes in sauna like heat whilst an ambulance stood empty outside. Outrageous! Thatcher's

Britain 1984. We know who the 'enemy within' really is after today.

We were kept waiting in that bloody van for over an hour and there was a puddle of sweat at my feet. The only thing that kept us amused was the fact that one of our fellow prisoners was the toilet cleaner from Dalkeith who had got carried along with the enthusiasm and found himself arrested. He kept saying, 'They can't arrest me. Ah'm no a miner. I'm in NUPE'! He amused me and Butch anyway.

We were eventually taken up the road to Dalkeith Police Station, photographed and charged, then put into cells. I had one to myself which was clean, with a toilet bowl in the corner and a thin mattress along one wall, opposite the grey door. The only light came weakly through thick glass tiles and I regretted having taken off my shirt because it was quite chilly. I lay on the thin mattress and tried to get some sleep, though my head and ribs were aching badly. I had a cut on my head and a black eye.

I was roused from my attempt by Butch calling my name. I went to the hatch in the door, which had been left open, and looked out. At another hatch to my right I could see Butch grinning like a loony, proudly displaying a pig's silver button. I couldn't believe his nerve and had to laugh when I tried to imagine where he had hid it when we got searched. Butch is a good laugh, and a good picket and he cheered me up a bit.

I was lying down again when I heard voices and a key turn in the lock. I jumped to my feet as two Westoe lads were shoved into the cell, Geordie Allen and John Scott. They told me there were 12 Westoe lads in the cells and we spent ages talking about what we'd seen and heard. Geordie Pape's son had been taken to hospital and his dad was really worried about him until he was brought to the cells a couple of hours later, bruised and battered, but fine. I got bored and started to write my name on the cell wall. Geordie and Tom were laughing at my gyrations and asked what the hell I was writing with. They laughed when I showed them my fly zipper!

We were finally fed by a policewoman at 6.30 who shoved three paper plates of fishcake, chips and peas through the hatch, and some lemonade supplied by the NUM and 3 cigarettes. I was so hungry I almost ate the plate as well. As John and me smoked our fag, and shared Geordie's cos he doesn't smoke, Geordie shouted for seconds through the hatch, and we were gobsmacked when three more plates of food were passed through. Geordie started on his but John and me held back feeling sure they'd made a mistake. However, hunger got the better of us and we gobbled up the warm food, giggling like loonies between gobfulls of food. I heard a gruff Scots voice calling to us so I went to the hatch. An angry looking Scotsman shouted,'Yous Geordie bastards have eaten wor dinner.' I ducked down to tell the others and we couldn't help laughing whilst the Scotsman's protests got louder. We heard him arguing with the policewoman that the men in his cell had not been fed, with her shouting back that 33 meals had been served so they must have been. It was only after the pigs had searched the cell for empty plates and found none that the lads finally got their food.

We were released at 8.30 and told that although we were free to picket we would be banned from every picket line in Britain if we get lifted again. He also told us that we would hear by post when we are due to appear in court.

We had a few pints and then headed for an early night to be ready for the morning picket.

Thursday July 26th, 1984
The early picket at Bilston Glen was the most militant so far but there was no attempt to form up for a push. Instead everyone seemed content to throw stones and bottles at the police lines to get revenge for yesterday. News came through that a coachload of Durham miners had been arrested in Tranent for allegedly harassing a scab and everyone seemed to go mental. Lads began tearing down the fence outside the pit yard which the NCB had spent thousands on having strengthened. Huge tyres were rolled over from a nearby garage and then set on fire, and within minutes thick black smoke was belching out from the flames and two trees had also caught alight. Missiles kept flying into the police lines.

A fire engine roared up, siren howling, but we formed a line across the road and Keith Smoult asked the firemen not to cross our 'official picket line'. They agreed and turned their engine around and drove off to massive cheers from the pickets and looks of disgust from the pigs. The stoning continued until bus loads of pigs began to arrive and we beat a tactical retreat.

Back on our coach we were told we were off to Dalkeith police station to protest about the arrest of our lads in Tranent. As soon as we arrived we piled off the coach to join the large crowd gathering at the top of the bank that ran up to the station. No sooner had we got there when we were scattered by pigs coming straight for us with truncheons drawn. It was a mad stampede for safety with the pigs tripping anyone that got too close to them. I managed to reach our coach and jumped on, gasping for breath. About a dozen lads had got there before me and they lined the windows watching the chaotic scenes outside. I could see a group of our lads hemmed in by the pigs so I ran a few yards and shouted to let them know where we were. A pig yelled at me to, 'Get back on the fuckin' bus or you're nicked'. He pushed me forward and I had no choice. He told the driver to leave immediately, even though most of our lads were missing. Fortunately none of them was arrested and they managed to get back in time for the afternoon picket.

It was a very subdued picket, with the highpoint being the Tranent Lodge

Banner being marched right up in front of the police as an act of defiance. Unfortunately that won't stop the scabs. Only mass pickets will.

We all went for a final drink in the Miners Welfare and there was a strong rumour flying around that the Scottish officials have signed a deal with the pigs to reduce picketing. More resentment has been caused by a Scottish picket being overheard saying this morning, 'Let the Durham lads go in front. They're getting paid for it.' Yeah, 170 Durham men arrested at Bilston Glen, that's what we paid!! Let's hope the rumours are untrue, and let's hope if they are, then the Scots lads can organise the picket over the heads of their weak officials, otherwise it will all have been for nothing.

At about eleven we were told that the final picket will be at 2.30am and it's all top secret. Most of the lads are too pissed to notice.

Friday July 27th, 1984

The 'top secret' picket was a bloody farce and achieved nothing more than costing those of us daft enough to turn out a night's sleep! Only one thing brightened up an otherwise useless picket and that was the sight of one of our lads, Brian, turning up pissed with all his gear in a carrier bag because he'd been told we were leaving straight afterwards. He was so pissed that when one of the lads took his bag he assumed they were putting it on the coach for him. They weren't, as we saw another lad stagger towards the entrance trying to pretend he was a scab going into work. He might have got away with it if it hadn't of been 3am and him staggering so much! As it was, him and Brian's full wardrobe were arrested, both being released at 5.30. This could have a lot to do with the smell from Brian's socks!

Back in Penicuik we said our goodbyes to Willie and Marlene, and an official thanked us for coming but said we wouldn't be needed in Scotland again. I guess this proves that a deal has been done, which is a depressing thought. How the hell can we win when our own union doesn't support us?

Kath and the girls were shocked when I got home and they saw all my bruises and cuts. I've had to promise to spend some time with them until I recover. I need a rest.

Tuesday July 31st, 1984

South Wales NUM have been fined £50,000 by the Tory courts and their assets have been seized for contempt of court. What else can anyone have but contempt for a system run by the ruling class for the ruling class? Surely this action will spur the rest of the TUC into the fight to support us. Not before bloody time!

I'm frustrated at being out of action but for once I have to pay attention to my family. Mind you, I did manage to go along to a picket at Steetly Quarry, County Durham, this morning by telling Kath there would be no trouble. No one seemed to know why we were there other than Dolomite, used in steelmaking, was being stored there along with Polish coal. There were about 700 men present and we managed to stop all the lorries going in. The picket was broken up by rumours of riot police being on their way. Bollocks, but at least we had a victory to celebrate.

Wednesday August 1st, 1984

I managed to get out again to attend a mass picket of about 700 men at the Philadelphia workshops to stop COSA scabs from going in. We failed miserably, mainly because not enough men were prepared to get involved.

Durham NUM seem to have adopted a new tactic of organising mass pickets at a different location every day. The theory is that this will confuse the police and keep them uncertain about our targets. The reality is that the pigs aren't that stupid and all we are achieving is preventing boredom amongst the pickets. We should just select a target and stick at it until we achieve our aim.

Also today Nigel Lawson revealed to the nation what most miners have known since day one of the strike, namely that the Tories are prepared to spend unlimited amounts of public money to defeat us. He said the cost of defeating us is 'a worthwhile investment for the good of the nation'. Surely people can now see the issue of the so called 'uneconomic pits' is a smokescreen to smash the unions!

Monday August 20th, 1984

Today was my first day back on picket duty after having time off to be with my family. The picket was at Westoe in case anyone was daft enough to fall for MacGregor's new 'back to work' plea. I ripped my letter up soon as it came through the letterbox. No one tried to work but I did manage to sell 15 copies of *Socialist Worker*. There were about 200 pickets on duty.

At Easington a lone scab tried to report for work but was prevented by over a thousand pickets, which is excellent, especially as a lot of the community turned out to support the miners. Of course the media are hailing him as a hero and are urging him to try again tomorrow and ignore the intimidation. I saw the bastard on the local news, Wilkinson he's called, and he doesn't look or sound like a 'full shilling' to me. He's the first scab in the North East and let's hope he's the last.

At Wearmouth Colliery 15 scabs, all COSA members, went in to work and took everyone by surprise. A mass picket has been called for the morning to try and nip the scabbing in the bud.

Tuesday August 21st, 1984
The mass picket at Wearmouth was a fiasco, with only about 250 pickets facing over 500 pigs. The scab at Easington has split our forces and a lot of the men at Wearmouth were arguing that Easington is more important because it's a NUM member involved. I tried to argue against them, saying 15 scabs could easily turn into 50 and then snowball from there. All scabbing has to be stopped and we should be asking for other unions to join us on the picket line instead of arguing over which one is more important.

Anyway 36 men were arrested at Wearmouth when the scab bus arrived. This is because the pickets are herded into a car park that has a shin high metal barrier surrounding it so we can't push forward. The other thing that wound us up was that the bus that took the scabs in comes from Easington. We've been assured that it won't be used tomorrow.

Down at Easington there was what the media called a 'riot', with cars belonging to management being overturned in the pit yard and windows smashed. It was a rare victory for us.

Wednesday August 22nd, 1984
An extra scab went into Wearmouth this morning and yet again we failed to stop the bus going in. The bastards were driven in on a Northern General Transport bus driven by a TGWU driver from the local depot. This really infuriated the pickets and men leapt over the barrier to try and get at the scabs. 9 men were arrested, including Keith Smoult.

A lot of the lads have been on to the Wearmouth officials to have the barrier round the car park removed at night. Lots of lads have been injured by that bloody fence and it really helps the pigs to keep control. It must be taken down.

Another national dock strike seems imminent due to scab labour being used at the Hunterston coal terminal in Scotland. Let's hope the bastards stick it out this time.

Thursday August 23rd, 1984
The bloody fence was still there when we arrived at Wearmouth this morning so someone suggested we blockade the nearby Wear bridge to highlight what was happening at Wearmouth. We all started to march off up the road to cut off the rush hour traffic into Sunderland at 8.15. As we set off the pigs stayed where they were, hundreds of them, probably because they thought it was a tactic to draw them away. Just before we reached the bridge two motorcycle cops tried to block our progress. Someone lobbed a brick which hit one of the pigs on his crash helmet, causing the stupid bastard to lunge himself into a crowd of pickets in a vain attempt to nick the culprit. Unfortunately for him he

tripped over an outstretched leg and crashed heavily to the ground where he lay apparently unconscious until someone stubbed their toe against his crash helmet, causing him to jump to his feet. When he saw he was on his own he fell down unconscious again. We marched past him, content that he had been given a small dose of his own medicine.

We stopped all the traffic but then men began to drift off towards the shipyards, enjoying the freedom to roam, stoning any police vehicle foolish enough to get too close. A car driver wound down his window and warned us that there was a large body of police waiting for us up the road so we cut off down a side road that brought us out opposite the police station and the DHSS. Within minutes there wasn't a pane of glass left in either building. Unfortunately the pigs organised and charged at us, splitting us into two groups. I was lucky enough to stay with the largest group and avoided capture. The other group was not so lucky, with 13 arrests being made. One of the Westoe lads was chased down by the river by 3 pigs and was overjoyed when shipyard workers came out and started pelting the pigs with nuts and bolts, forcing them to retreat! Now that's solidarity for you, and it DOES work.

The media have had a field day, calling us thugs and hooligans, and reported that, 'A brave motorcycle policeman was dragged from his bike and beaten unconscious by violent thugs.' We know the truth and people should realise that what happened this morning was a reaction to all the shit miners and their families have been suffering for months.

The dock strike is on and already the media are trying to undermine it by calling it a set up job between Scargill and the TGWU leaders, and calling on 'responsible' dockers to scab. Bastards!!

MacGregor has offered the scabs a 5.2% pay rise if they agree to work overtime. I expect they'll take it.

Friday August 24th, 1984

Wearmouth again and that bloody fence is still there. Despite it we had a good push and almost stopped the police van taking the scabs in. Only eleven of the bastards went in today and that proves picketing works if it's sustained. 26 arrests though, which isn't good.

The lads down in Easington are having it really rough and riot police have virtually cut the place off. Men are being arrested for nothing and known militants are being beaten up. People's houses are being invaded for no reason and the place is full of police in full riot gear. Thatcher's Britain 1984! When are people going to take notice of what is going on in their own country? Dangerous precedents are being set. It's us miners today but it could easily be the rest of the workers turn next if we don't start getting the support we so desperately need.

Thursday August 30th, 1984
No picket at Wearmouth today because their leader, a twat called Seed, had promised they wouldn't go in if there were only 6 official pickets on duty. The officials agreed and we were sent to Monkton Coke Works near Jarrow where a lone scab had crawled out of his dung heap

We made a real attempt to stop him going in but the pigs were far better organised and 11 men were arrested. The pigs were vicious and the Monkton men had their first bitter taste of state violence.

The arrested men were dealt with very harshly by the Tory court and have been banned from every picket line in the British Isles! This is astonishing when you consider it was the first ever arrest for most of the men and they were only charged with Obstruction of the Highway. Local Labour MPs expressed their shock. Where have they been for the past 6 months?

Whilst we were fighting the pigs at Monkton, Seed and his mates went into work as usual, informing the official picket that that they meant 6 pickets at every pit in the country. Bastards! We won't get fooled again, I hope.

Friday August 31st, 1984
Today saw the first appearance of the new scab bus. Unbelievable! It must have cost a bloody fortune. It has silvered windows covered in heavy steel mesh and painted grey. The most expensive rat cage ever!

We had plenty of pickets but no organisation, and no commitment; the men just seemed content to shout abuse at the scabs going in, hidden behind their silvered windows. I'm getting fed up with the lack of action and often wonder whether it's worth turning out.

Monday September 3rd, 1984
The TUC Conference opened in Brighton today and was lobbied by a large crowd of miners and their supporters, despite fears of a massive back to work movement in the coalfields.

Scargill was given a tremendous reception when he took the stage to speak to the delegates. He gave his usual fiery defiant speech which got a great reception. The rest of the TUC Mafia gave him verbal support, but rhetoric is one thing, and action is another. They've promised to support us but I'll only believe it when I see it, if I see it!

The picket at Westoe was very quiet and no one tried to go in. A lot of men are getting pissed off with the regular Monday picket but I think we have to keep doing it to put off any potential scabs.

Kath has been told by her bosses that if she wants to stay in her job as Warden of the Women's Aid Refuge she must take her chance with other people and reapply for her job. She is very upset at this because she's done a great job. I think she is being picked on because one of her bosses on the board that runs the place just happens to be a policewoman, and Kath's the wife of a striking miner. I hope I'm wrong because it's not helping our marriage. Whatever happens we'll manage. We'll have to!

Tuesday September 4th, 1984

The picket at Wearmouth this morning was the most frustrating yet. We had plenty of men, over 200, but no enthusiasm or commitment. I did try to organise but no one took any notice of me and I gave up. I put this down to false optimism after yesterday's TUC resolution. A lot of men now think the end's in sight, just as they did during the dockers' short lived revolt. I am more pessimistic and feel there is no way Thatcher is going let Scargill have any kind of victory. We need the lights to go out and lots of support from other workers.

PRISON NOTES

Wednesday September 5th, 1984
I am actually writing this diary on Saturday September 8th after having spent the last 3 days in Durham prison.

The day began at 7am when I left the Armstrong Hall in Neil Tate's car to go picketing at Wearmouth as usual. I told the lads I was with that we should not just stand around being passive but needed to take some positive action. They all agreed.

We arrived at Wearmouth at 7.30 and joined the fifty or so men already in the car park. I had a chat with Dave Hopper, the Lodge Secretary of Wearmouth, and asked him why the fence hadn't been removed because it was a real hindrance to us having a proper push against the pigs. Dave agreed with me but said there was nothing he could do because the pigs were at the pit 24 hours a day. He also told me that Sunderland Magistrates were taking a really hard line with arrested pickets. Two of his lads had been remanded in custody to Durham prison. I know one of them really well, Alan Margham, and I asked Dave to pass him my regards when he saw him. Little did I know that I would see him before he did!

By 7.45 there were at least 250 of us in the car park facing a line of about 200 pigs directly in front of the main pit entrance, separated by the bloody metal fence. A group of us began moving around the picket because we were really pissed off with the passivity. After having had men lifted on a daily basis the hard core activists were also being reduced, and the picket had become really stale. We couldn't allow it to continue because a passive picket would just encourage more scabbing. We started telling the lads we were going out onto the road on our right to form a push and asked everyone to join us.

Accordingly about twenty of us moved onto the road and began shouting for everyone to join us. We soon had about a hundred men but the majority refused to move, even when we yelled at them and called them 'plastic pickets' and worse. I have a big gob and my throat hurt with the effort of shouting but it did no good.

The scab bus was due so we formed up into a solid mass and started to move towards the pigs, who had rushed to form a reinforced line in front of us. We chanted our battle cry of 'Zulu, Zulu, Zulu' and then crashed into the pigs. Initially we made progress, forcing the pigs back a little until more reinforcements joined their lines. We could have broken through easily if the 'plastics' watching from the sidelines had joined us. As it was the push was broken by a group of pigs attacking from the side and splitting off the front two lines from the rest of the lads. I was roughly grabbed around the throat by a pig and struggled to fight back and keep my feet. The bastard was choking me and he dragged me through the police lines. He threw me to the ground, and as I struggled to get my breath he leapt on me with his knee across my chest. I could see he was an inspector by his flat hat and he said, 'Got you at last, you big mouthed bastard. That's your picketing days over.' I wondered if I'd been singled out as I was roughly dragged backwards and thrown into the back of a police van. Within minutes the van was full, with 8 pickets and six pigs, and we were driven the short distance over the bridge to the same police station we had stoned the week before.

Inside Monkwearmouth police station, which was so small it didn't have any cells, with my 'arresting officer', a young PC, we were told to stand against the wall to have our photograph taken by an obese sergeant (is there any other kind?) with a Polaroid camera. He told me the photo was for 'official' records, ie the photo albums they used to identify activists. The sergeant pressed the button and all four flash cubes went off and unexposed film shot out the front. I laughed out loud and so did the young PC but the sergeant wasn't amused. Cursing, he fitted new flashes and loaded new film. We composed ourselves, with me trying to look defiant and the PC smiling broadly. The same thing happened, flashes and film spewing out of the front. I was laughing madly when an angry Inspector burst into the room and demanded to know what the hell was going on! The fat sergeant said he couldn't understand it because it had never happened before. He tried one more time with exactly the same result. The Inspector grabbed the camera and threw it in a bin and ordered the sergeant to go and get a replacement.

Finally I was photographed and then taken into another room where the angry Inspector was waiting impatiently. He said to the PC, 'What kind of abusive language did this scum use?' The young lad was either very naïve, very stupid, or a mixture of the two because he replied, 'Sorry sir, but I didn't actually hear him say anything.' I thought the Inspector was going to explode. He yelled for the fat sergeant to take me away. As I was being taken out I heard the Inspector say, 'Now what did you hear the bastard say?' No doubt that cleared the young lad's memory.

I was taken outside and locked into a tiny cell on one of them pig buses you usually see parked at football grounds. An uncomfortable hour later there were 12 of us in the cells and we were driven to Gill Bridge police station in Sunderland and locked in two cells, six to a cell. I was with 3 Westoe lads, one of whom had only been doing picket duty for a fortnight! I grew up in the same street as one of the lads, Davy Larsen, and we spent the time chatting about our experiences over the past 6 months.

During the morning we were taken out to be photographed, again, fingerprinted and questioned, and finally charged. I was charged with 'Foul, insulting and abusive behaviour liable to cause a breach of the peace'. The officer charging me asked if I had any outstanding charges against me and he grinned when I told him about Bilston Glen last month.

We were allowed to see a solicitor provided by the NUM and he told me that we would probably be bailed and banned from going within two miles of Wearmouth, which is what I was expecting.

We had dinner of soya pie, potato and turnip, which was bloody horrible but I ate it anyway. We were then let out of the cells and told to wait at the foot of the stairs that led up into the courtroom. We whispered amongst ourselves. I recognised one of the lads, Bob Robson, who had been one of the most vociferous supporters of going to jail in Bishop Auckland but had bottled out and phoned the TV instead. He got me worried when he told me the solicitor who had seen him had warned him he might be refused bail and be remanded in custody because of his previous arrest. This had happened to men who had appeared before the bench previously. It wasn't looking good. I was feeling a bit pissed off because he had seen a woman, as had most of the other lads, with only a few of us seeing the man. I suspected he must be a trainee or something because he told me I would probably be bailed.

It was 3pm when the first six lads were led up into the court, and when they came back they told us that they had been bailed and weren't allowed to go within two miles of Wearmouth, as they'd expected. We were called up and I was a bit surprised when the magistrate called the first four lads to the bench and left Bob and me to one side. The lads were all released on the same bail conditions as the other six.

We were ordered to face the magistrate and he glared at us as if we were two lumps of shit. Bob was dealt with first, and despite the pleas of our female solicitor, was remanded in custody in Durham prison until September 14th. Bob was led down, looking totally shocked. I faced the magistrate and received the same sentence with the magistrate saying I was being remanded because of my disgraceful past record and that he believed I would ignore any bail conditions imposed on me. He also said something about me being a danger to public order but I was too gobsmacked to take it all in. What evidence did the bastard have that I would ignore bail conditions? He ordered me to be taken down and the guy who led me away said the time would soon pass. Easy for him to say. He wasn't going to Durham Prison!

After being held in a cell for half an hour we were taken up to a yard and handcuffed together before being put into a van. It was an uncomfortable journey, made worse by the gobshite sergeant who accompanied us. He was one of those, 'some of my best friends are miners' types and was constantly trying to be friendly. I ignored the bastard but Bob chatted happily with him. The pig was condemning Scargill and the picket line violence, and Bob was agreeing with him! I couldn't believe it and wondered why he'd been on the picket line in the first place. Bob said he couldn't wait to get back to work and that it would soon happen because there was no way we could defeat Thatcher. It made an already depressing journey worse and I worried about what Kath would say when she found out, and how Jen and Sasha would react. I was also angry that none of our union officials had been in court so how would Kath find out? I hoped Keith or Gary would call round to tell her. I felt as if I was about to start a life sentence instead of a few days on remand and resolved that in the future I would content myself with being an 'indian' and leave being 'chief' to others.

Once inside the prison gates the handcuffs were taken off and we were taken into the Search Tank, which is a room beside the main gate where incoming prisoners are taken to be searched. They searched everywhere, even the soles of my feet, and it was a humiliating experience. After the usual jokes about my surname we were taken into the reception area, and after another lengthy wait we were taken into another room where we were told to strip naked. Then we were taken into another room full of men waiting to be admitted into the prison. One of these men was a long term prisoner who was being transferred to a prison in Scotland. He told me he's been in Wakefield prison for seven years and this was the first time in all those years he'd been outside. He told me he was doing life for murder, yet despite this I felt quite sorry for him. The other men were burglars and con men who passed the time bragging about the crimes they'd gotten away with before being caught for something trivial. When they heard what Bob and me were in for they were very sympathetic and gave us loads of advice on what to expect and what we could get away with. Bob said he'd done some time as a younger man and started telling tales of his exploits as a criminal, trying to be the equal of the other men, daft bastard. He's a bit of a know all is Bob. Anyway, I was glad for the advice and felt a bit easier in my mind.

We were examined by the prison doctor before being forced to have a bath in cold water full of disinfectant. The towel I dried on was like sandpaper. We were then issued with our uniform; one pair of underpants, one vest, a pair of socks with holes in the heels, a blue striped shirt, a brown pair of trousers that were too big, and a brown jacket stamped with 'HMP Durham' in case anyone tried to nick it. The whole outfit was completed by a pair of battered black slip-on shoes, with mine having holes gouged in the heels, making it uncomfortable to walk, not that I expected to be doing a lot of that!

Dressed, washed and given a number, all we had to look forward to was prison food. I was bloody starving but when I saw what was on offer I almost lost my appetite. I was handed a plate with a blob of mashed potato, shrivelled up peas and a solitary hot dog sausage. A plastic mug of unsweetened tea was provided, presumably to wash away the horrible taste of the food which I had gulped down with a minimum of chewing in the hope that my taste buds wouldn't be irreparably damaged.

After our meal we had another long wait. I passed the time chatting with a con man who was on a three year sentence, and if he was to be believed, had £30,000 stashed for his release. He entertained me with stories of his many criminal exploits and the time passed quickly. He also gave me some cigarettes and it was great to have a smoke because I had finished the few I was given back when we came to Durham. I am grateful to the 'screw' who gave me them because prison rules stated that only sealed packets should be given back. He told me he supported the miners, which came as a pleasant surprise because I had expected the screws to be bastards like the police are. In fact, all the screws we had contact with were great, with one in particular, being an ex-miner himself, doing all he could to make our stay less uncomfortable.

Bob and I were to be kept together, which came as a relief because I'd heard all the tales of homosexuality in prisons. Not that I've anything against homosexuals. I just didn't want to experience it first hand! At 9pm we were given a sheet, a pillowcase and a blanket. We carried these into B wing because the remand wing was full. We climbed the metal staircase and I thought of the prison in *Porridge*. There was thick wire mesh strung beneath the landings to stop men throwing themselves off to escape the food! We were on the second floor, in cell B2-30, and it was really depressing when we went in and the door was locked behind us.

Our cell was bloody horrible. It was filthy, with fag ends on the cracked concrete floor. The arch window had thick glass panes that were filthy, and six of them were missing, causing a chill breeze to waft around the cell and circulate the stink from the plastic bucket full of piss and shit that stood in the middle. The décor was post-holocaust, damp grey walls and cobwebbed ceiling. We each had a metal frame bed with a thin white mattress that was full of stains, and mine was also covered with a school boyish drawing of a naked woman in blue biro. We also had a blue plastic mug each, an orange plastic washing bowl and jug, and a plastic razor with no blade. Two wooden tables completed the furniture, all crammed into a cell no more than six foot wide, and twelve long.

The screw, who Bob kept calling 'Boss', told us to make a final trip to the bog. The first thing I saw on entering was a contorted face behind a half door, complete with sound effects as he strained to shit. He put me right off and I was determined to hold my bowels for as long as I could.

Back in the cell Bob was the first to spot two books and immediately claimed the cowboy book. I was relieved until I saw the other book was a biography of Martin Luther. I skimmed it and quickly decided it wasn't for me. I would have happily swapped it for the cowboy book.

At 10pm the light went out and we settled down to sleep. I was knackered but it took me a long time to drop off. I worried about Kath and the girls, and for me that is the worst thing about being locked up, not being able to communicate with your loved ones and not knowing what is happening to them.

Thursday September 6th, 1984

I got woken up just after 4am by the bloody bells of Durham Cathedral. It came as quite a shock to realise I wasn't having a nightmare and that I really was in a filthy stinking cell in Durham prison. I tried to get back to sleep but couldn't so I was relieved when the cell light went on at six. I got dressed and lay on my bed waiting for Bob to wake up.

At 6.30 our cell door was opened and the screw gave us each a razor blade wrapped in paper, and allowed us to get hot water from the toilet. I unwrapped my blade and had a shave, using the paper to cover the numerous cuts I had inflicted upon myself. I was surprised when the screw returned for the razor blade, which had to be put into a slot in a clipboard marked with my number. The screw said I should have kept the paper but it didn't matter because I was the only one who would use the blade. Bob of course, being an old lag, did keep his paper and told me I would have to use the same blade for a month. If I'm still here I'll grow a beard!

At 7am I went downstairs to get breakfast but Bob stuck to his resolution not to eat anything and stayed in the cell. After eating the lukewarm baked beans on half a slice of fried bread, and a slice of bread with the most disgusting tasting margarine, I wished I had his willpower! I tried to get rid of the taste with half a mug of sugarless tea but I still felt ill. At 7.30 I put the empty tray outside the cell door and then dozed fitfully whilst Bob read his cowboy book.

Just after nine our cell door was opened and we were taken down to the reception area to see our solicitor. On the way we passed Alan Margham from Wearmouth but only had time to say a quick hello before we were out. Still, it was nice to know we weren't alone.

Bob saw the solicitor first and spent an hour and forty minutes talking to him and smoking his fags. I spent the time listening to the conversations of other prisoners which was almost exclusively about their criminal careers, which ranged from car theft to attempted murder! I was relieved when my turn came.

My relief was short lived because the first thing he told me was that we would not be released today, which is what I'd been hoping for. He explained that an appeal would be made to a Judge in Chambers, but before this could be done I had to make a full statement about almost every aspect of my private life, the effect my remand would have on my wife and children, and the effect it would have on my widowed mother. The short time I had been in prison had a profound effect on me and I would have said anything to get out. How different from the protest at Bishop Auckland only a few months ago. At eleven the solicitor had to leave because of prison regulations and I cursed Bob for taking so long. I didn't have enough time to give as full a statement as I would've liked and felt quite resentful towards him. The solicitor was very apologetic and assured me he would do his best to have us released before the weekend.

We were taken back to our cell and locked up again. I was let out at 12 to go and get some dinner but it tasted so disgusting I left most of it on the tray, despite my hunger. Bob still refused.

At 2.30 Bob was taken down for a visit and I felt really depressed that no one had come to see me. I was even more depressed when Bob returned loaded down with cigarettes, chocolates and fruit juice, some of which was brought by Lodge officials from his pit, Wearmouth, the rest from his wife. Where was Kath? If his officials could visit, where the bloody hell were the Westoe officials? I was absolutely furious that they couldn't even take the trouble to visit, or even arrange for Kath to visit. Bastards!

The rest of the day was spent locked up and I declined supper because I was too angry to eat. Bob shared his stuff with me and we spent the time till lights out talking about the strike. I couldn't believe how conservative Bob was in his views, and I couldn't for the life of me understand how he ever came to be on a picket line, let alone be sharing a prison cell with me. He said we should have had a ballot, mass pickets were futile, and we should just get back to work! I argued with him, shouted at him but it was futile. There was no way I could change his mind.

He does have one strong point though. He isn't squeamish like me and emptied the bucket full of piss and shit left by the previous occupants, improving the quality of air in our cell. I will always be grateful to him for that!

Friday September 7th, 1984

I slept badly and was woken at 5am by those bloody church bells ringing like some giant alarm clock! A curse on religion.

We went through the same routine as yesterday but the breakfast was worse, one hot dog sausage, tea and bread, no margarine after yesterday's first and last taste.

At 10 we were given a choice of activity. We could either spend an hour walking round the exercise yard, Bob chose that, or an hour and a half of sport, which I chose, hoping I would exhaust myself enough to get some sleep.

About 15 of us were taken across to a gym where we were given another choice, do weights or play football. I chose football so we carried two sets of goals out onto a tarmac covered area surrounded by high fencing, and split into two teams of four.

We started to play and it was very competitive. After about 15 minutes I was knackered. There was this big bloke covered in tattoos and I stuck out my foot to tackle him. Unfortunately I mistimed it and tripped the bloke up, causing him to go scudding across the tarmac on his knees, skinning them badly. Despite that he leapt to his feet and came at me, calling me 'a fat fuckin' cunt' and threatening to kill me. Screws came from all directions and held him back and tried to calm him down. The screw who was refereeing came to me and said,' Better steer clear of him, son! He's murdered two already so one more won't make any difference.' To be honest I was terrified, and spent the remainder of the game running in the opposite direction whenever he came near me. I was relieved when we were taken back to our cells and vowed that in the future I would walk round in circles with Bob.

I had dinner at 12 and as expected it was disgusting, but I still cleared my plate. No doubt you could get used to it but I'm certain no one could ever say they enjoyed it. After all, we were there to be punished and eating certainly rammed that point home!

After dinner Bob and me discussed our chances of release. Three miners had been released yesterday and Bob's hopes were pinned on him going today. He said he couldn't stand another day inside, let alone a weekend. I was a lot more pessimistic about my own chances and was resigned to spending the weekend inside. If I was released then that would be a bonus.

My pessimism seemed justified when the screw let Bob out at 2.15 for another visit, and I felt deserted and alone as I sat in the cell and cursed my Lodge officials. I jumped when I heard the door being opened at three, thinking it was Bob returning but the screw informed me I had a visitor, Mrs Callan. As we made our way downstairs I guessed that Mrs Callan was the wife of our Area Secretary and wondered why she'd been sent to visit me. At least it would be contact with the outside world.

I was taken to the reception area and told to wait until I was called. My name was called and I went into a room with a long line of tables running the entire length. I was taken to the middle and couldn't believe my eyes when I saw Kath sitting there and all we could do was just stare lovingly at each other. We both tried to talk at once but were interrupted by the arrival of Tommy Callan, his wife, and John Chapman, our Lodge Chairman., who was full of lame excuses for not coming earlier. I listened to them impatiently until they took the hint and left us alone. Kath told me that I would almost certainly be released today because the solicitor was appearing before the Judge in Chambers at 2.30. She was shocked at seeing me in a prison uniform, and by the whole degrading process of visiting someone in prison. A screw came up and told us our 15 minutes were up and asked Kath to leave. She told me she'd left some cigarettes and two cans of lager, and said she hoped she'd see me later. I hoped so too!

After I was given my goods, which included a box of chocolates from Mrs Callan, I was locked back up in the cell. I ate all the soft centres from the chocolates whilst Bob paced up and down the cell, driving me nuts with his patter, saying he was getting out for certain but that I would probably have to remain on remand because of my previous record. He said that this was Tommy Callan's view as well and I began to get really depressed. Suddenly the cell door was opened and the screw said, 'Come on, lads, you're out on bail.' I could've kissed him I was so relieved. We got our stuff and headed down the stairs. The warder kindly allowed us to give our chocolate and cigarettes to two lads from Blyth whom Bob had befriended somehow and they were overjoyed to get them. In prison terms they were rich.

We were given our own clothes to change back into and had to sign for our things in a big envelope. When I opened mine to check it I found £17.70p which puzzled me because I'd only been lifted with the 70p! Bob also had £17 extra and we wondered whether we should say something because maybe they were trying to trick us so they could keep us in. We agreed to sign and then sat down and waited for the arrival of the Chief Warder with our bail forms. He solved the puzzle by saying, 'As a Yorkshireman I support your fight but disagree with the violence. We had a collection amongst the warders and the extra money is to take your wives out for a nice meal.' I was genuinely touched by this show of support and thanked him. He said he hoped he'd never see either of us again and then got us to sign the bail forms. Mine said, 'The defendant is not to go within 200 yards of any NCB premises where picketing is taking place except to go to work in the normal course, and to attend the DHSS office at Monkwearmouth between the hours of 10am – 4pm.' I would have signed anything, even though I was effectively banned from picketing. I breathed a huge sigh of relief as we walked out of the main gate at 6pm. You'd think I'd just done 3 years, not 3 days.

Bob's sister dropped him off and then was kind enough to drop me off at home. Kath and me were overjoyed to see each other and the girls were embarrassed as we kissed and hugged. Later, after we'd eaten a delicious meal and I'd put the girls to bed, Kath told me of the struggle she'd had to get the Lodge to visit me. She even had to find out the visiting times herself! The only help she'd got from the Lodge was a lift to and from Durham, and she said that in her opinion none of the bastards seemed bothered I was in prison. That didn't particularly surprise me given other events, but what did have me fuming was the pressure Kath had been put under by those bastards. She has enough shit to cope with without men who are supposed to be on my side adding to it. I intend raising it at the next Lodge meeting, if only so other lads don't suffer in the same way.

Catching up on the news I find that Kneel Kinnock spoke at the TUC Conference on September 5th, the day we were jailed. He said, 'Violence creates a climate of brutality. It is alien to the temperament and the intelligence of the British union movement.' What a load of bollocks! How the hell does he think we got unions in the first place? By asking our lords and masters for permission? NO, through the blood of thousands of workers in the past who fought to get them. Even bloody Thatcher has the Suffragettes to thank for using violence at times to get the vote. If we have to rely on shits like Kinnock then we will lose everything our ancestors paid for with their blood. Fuck Kinnock, and his softy lefty mates. I for one will fight to keep those rights, and build on them, and so will millions of others.

A journalist from the *New Musical Express* rang and has asked if he can stay with us for a few days to write an article about the strike. Kath has agreed and he will arrive tomorrow night.

KEEP ON KEEPIN' ON

Sunday September 9th, 1984
I had intended staying at home today with Kath but we had a blazing row so I went to Doncaster for an SWP miners meeting instead. I'm glad I did because it gave us the opportunity to discuss how the strike is going in our respective areas. There was general agreement that the strike is now firmly on the defensive, with all of us mainly concerned with stopping scabs breaking the strike. To ensure this we need to get more men onto the picket lines, and as Ian Mitchell from Silverwood told us from his own experience, the way to do that is to 'go on the knocker' and visit every striking miner and argue why they should be active. At the very least it could prevent men from scabbing, which will be important if we are to go on the offensive in the winter.

There was also agreement that there is a big danger of the new talks between MacGregor and Scargill leading to a sell out, and further demoralisation if they break down, which seems inevitable because the NUM has nothing to bargain with. We haven't got the bastards by the balls, nowhere near it.

The importance of us selling *Socialist Worker* was stressed again and again because that is how pickets can be kept informed of exactly what is happening in the strike. We must always try to sell the paper on picket lines, in welfares and strike centres because it's vital we are identified with the paper. That's how we get our ideas across and we can have important arguments at the same time. At Westoe, Gary, Ian, John, Keith and myself have built a good reputation as active militants and we need to continue being identified with the SWP and put forward constructive suggestions at union meetings. The first one is to get a list of addresses and use all the men banned from picketing to go and visit men who are not active and persuade them to join us.

I got a phone call asking me to meet the journalist at the bus stop near our house and I set off, expecting to meet some hippie type with long hair and flares because I used to read the *NME* regularly up until a couple of years ago. I was shocked when a tall skinhead with a red Harrington jacket, jeans and red boxing boots loomed up out of the darkness. He introduced himself as Chris Moore and we walked back to my house. I was relieved to hear he's an SWP member and not in the National Front, as I'd always irrationally thought about skinheads.

We sat up talking about the strike and about music. He's in a band called 'The Redskins', whom I've never heard of, but he's brought me a record and tape of their stuff which I'll listen to tomorrow.

Monday September 10th, 1984

We woke up early and I took Chris down to the Westoe picket line and introduced him to some of the lads. No one tried to go in so still 100% solid.

We went round to Gary's house near the pit and had tea and toast. Chris interviewed Gary, but only after politely telling me to shut up because I was answering all the questions. We also visited Dave Farham who lives just down the road, and Chris made sure I didn't interrupt by doing the interview in the kitchen whilst I looked after Leah, Dave's baby daughter.

This evening I took Chris down to the 'Shack' in Boldon Colliery. The pit shut years ago and the land is now used to stockpile coal, thousands of tons of it. We tried to find some striking miners but were unsuccessful, not surprising really as buying food is more important than buying beer. Chris did manage to talk to two old men who remembered 1926 but their memories were mostly about the poverty in those days. One of them did mention a scab who had died in the 60s and no one came to his funeral bar the vicar. That's what'll happen to anyone who has the nerve to scab at Westoe!

We visited John, who had been really active at the start of the strike but then had just stopped coming. He seemed the perfect person to start our policy of getting more men on the picket line but when he told us he'd just spent £300 buying a dog I had grave doubts. However, he sounded keen and has promised to come to Wearmouth so we'll see. The picket at Wearmouth tomorrow has been set for 2pm, so perhaps something has been organised.

Chris and me were talking for ages before I left him to get some sleep. Early start tomorrow. I like his music because it's all political, no love songs.

Tuesday September 11th, 1984

We got up early this morning to travel down to Easington, a two bus journey via Sunderland, so Chris and me had loads of time to talk.

We had a brilliant time in Easington. First of all we visited Tommy Ashurst in his house. God, poor Tommy has suffered and lives in a threadbare house. He is a single miner and gets no help other than the support he gets from the local community yet he is as active and militant as he was on day one. He told Chris about how the village was totally surrounded by riot police when the scab went back, and how the pigs insulted and abused the local people. Shocking, and something I hope we never experience at Westoe. The visit renewed my faith in the strike and made me realise how lucky I am in comparison to Tommy.

At the soup kitchen we met the most inspirational woman I have ever met, Heather Woods, one of the women behind SEAM (Save Easington Area Mines). She actually has nothing to do with mining, her husband is a plumber, but as she says, it's her community and she will fight for it to survive. Heather helps to run 'The Miner's Kitchen' and they are serving 500 to 600 meals a day and doing a fantastic job. We need something like this at Westoe because it really brings people together.

Chris went to the Wearmouth picket on his own this afternoon because it was too risky for me to make an appearance. He told me the picket was sold out by Lodge officials and Bob Clay, left wing Labour MP and ex-revolutionary. Apparently over 300 pickets took the pigs completely by surprise and some of the men barricaded the front entrance whilst others started to rip up the barrier round the car park. They had the opportunity to occupy the whole pit and get at the scabs but that bloody stupid rumour about riot police and horses started again, and Bob Clay appealed to the pickets to leave, saying, 'We've achieved what we came to do', and he was supported by the officials! Chris is disgusted, as are most of the other militants I've spoken to on the phone. It was a wasted opportunity to stop the scabbing and send out a message to all those other bastards sitting at home thinking of joining them.

Chris has left for Yorkshire, and I really hope he finds them a lot better organised than we are in Durham.

Kath is on a real downer and keeps going on about losing her job. I've told her we'll cope if she does but it hasn't made any bloody difference.

Thursday September 13th, 1984

We had a union meeting this morning which was very stormy. I had a real go at the officials for the lackadaisical way they dealt with Kath when I was in prison and for not visiting earlier as Wearmouth had done. I also criticised the payment of £30 to the men who went down to Brighton to lobby the TUC. It's totally irresponsible to waste money so blatantly in the 27th week of the strike, especially as we need more money to increase picketing. For once the Secretary agreed with me on both points and has promised to look into it to make sure it doesn't happen again.

We got nothing but lame excuses when we asked for a list of names and addresses, such as we can't hassle men if they don't want to picket, and they know where to come if they do. This negative attitude fails to take into account the fact that a lot of our men live a long distance from the town and can't afford to come on picket duty. We could provide transport from Lodge funds, which haven't been touched yet, and never will be if the bastards on the stage are allowed to make the decisions. What's the point of having funds if there's no pit? Bloody short-sighted, the lot of them!

The one positive thing to come out of the meeting is we seem to be getting a good base of support amongst the lads and we need to build on that.

Friday September 14th, 1984

I appeared at Sunderland Magistrates Court and was yet again remanded on the same oppressive bail conditions until October 1st.

The latest round of talks between the NUM and the NCB look ready to break down again. In my opinion there's no point in talking to the bastards until we have them by the balls!

Tuesday September 18th, 1984

The bloody dock strike is over, sold out again, even worse than the last time. This won't do any good for the morale of the pickets, many of whom seem to build up their hopes of a settlement every time talks begin. They are really pissed off today by the dockers selling out. It's now more important than ever to get more men onto the picket line, and for us to sell the paper so that they can understand why we've been sold out, and how we can still win this strike if we go on the offensive in numbers. It can be done!

Wednesday September 19th, 1984

Fuckin' hell!! We have a scab at Westoe and all hell has broken loose around the pit, with riot police everywhere!

Apparently, at six o' clock this morning a man called Walker went into the pit through the back entrance where there were no pickets. It was only when the bastard came out at the end of his shift that the pickets realised he was scabbing. He only lives 50 yards from the pit so he was quickly besieged in his house by an ever increasing crowd of people, angry that one of their neighbours had betrayed all their hardship and suffering by breaking the strike.

The pigs started to arrive in full riot gear and without any warning they started to wade viciously into the crowd, kicking, punching and clubbing anyone unfortunate enough to be in their way. People were chased in all directions, men, women and children, with one old man of 70 being beaten to the ground, and his small dog, who was trying to protect him, was kicked over a wall. The pigs insulted women who came to their front doors to see what was going on, calling them 'filthy sluts', 'dirty cows', and 'whores' whilst their children screamed at their sides. It was horrifying and disgusting and totally over the top.

After having cleared the whole area the pigs ordered council workmen to tear down our picket hut, which had been provided by the local Labour council, flattening it despite pickets' personal belongings being inside.

12 arrests were made, including the local 'Lollipop Lady', and a man who collided with a passing pig when he was getting out of his car to visit his elderly mother. He's been charged with 'Obstructing the police', and rumour has it he is a member of the SDP. Perhaps he can tell 'Dr Death' about it and change his views about 'the hooligans on picket lines'.

Predictably the local TV news covered the pig riot, and in their view, everyone should support the poor scab who is merely exercising his right to work, and besides, his mother has a weak heart. So does her fuckin' son!

Let's hope that this disgusting display of thuggery by the police, and the scab who caused it, only goes to strengthen the resolve of the men not to be bullied back to work and make us all the more determined to stick it out.

Friday September 21st – Sunday September 23rd, 1984

What a bloody wasted weekend. I attended a school at Durham University organised by Broad Left groups in South Wales and Durham. There were a few hundred active pickets attending, and there was a real opportunity to discuss ways of putting the strike back on the offensive. Instead we had to sit through boring lectures on subjects most of us had experienced at first hand, ie the role of the media, the courts, and the police. It was more like a post-mortem, and I was really disappointed when a pratt called Kim Howells attacked the use of mass pickets at Orgreave and Port Talbot, and none of us were allowed to argue against him. I'm bloody mad at myself for going!

One thing that cheered us up was the controversial comments by the new Bishop of Durham who called MacGregor 'an imported elderly American', and upset the Tories, who have always believed that god is on their side. I even sold a copy of *Socialist Worker* to a passing clergyman.

Friday September 28th, 1984

Wonders will never cease! Those spineless bastards at NACODs have voted overwhelmingly to take strike action, 82% in favour, in response to the NCB's threat to stop their wages for not crossing picket lines. Let's wait and see if they have the guts to carry it out.

It's been a bad week because Kath has lost her job and today was her last day at work. She is devastated and can't understand why she didn't get the job. Oh well, we're in the same boat as the rest of the striking miners now and we'll just have to get on with it.

Also, I've been unable to get to the Westoe picket because of my bail conditions, and the whole area is awash with pigs. Too risky.

Monday October 1st, 1984

This afternoon I made my third appearance at Sunderland Magistrates Court on the 'Breach of the Peace' charge arising from my arrest at Wearmouth on September 5th. I have been remanded on the same bail conditions until December 18th!! This is typical of what is happening to hundreds of activists who are prevented from picketing by the Tory courts. Why aren't the NUM lawyers doing more to try and fight them?

I am really pissed off and frustrated by being out of action, especially now that the NCB is piling on the pressure to get men to break the strike. I'll just have to try and find new ways to channel my energy, back to fundraising, I expect.

The Labour Party Conference opened today and Scargill got a standing ovation. He was also served with a writ from the High Court that threatens him with jail if he won't comply. He says he won't, and he also criticised the pigs for their disgraceful part in trying to defeat us. Standing ovations are fine but it's the support of the TUC we need, not bloody empty hand clapping!

The situation at home is terrible, with Kath in a deep depression because she has lost her job. Nothing I say does any good; she just sits and mopes. Hopefully she will get over it and find another job, though with unemployment rife she is going to find it hard. At least we're still together and perhaps now she can get more involved in the strike.

Tuesday October 2nd, 1984

Kinnock's speech today to the Labour Conference was a bloody disgrace! Yet again he bleated on about his hatred of violence and said the law must be obeyed. He should have been at Westoe last week, or Easington so he can see where the violence is really coming from! The bastard is just trying to curry favour with the middle classes so Labour can get elected. If he is on the side of the working class then I'm a Dutchman. Anyone who believes that a Labour Government under Kinnock and Hattersley will be vastly different from Thatcher's Junta is living in cloud cuckoo land!

The NCB has threatened to close Wearmouth if men are not allowed in to do 'vital' safety work. To their credit the union officials have refused unless the scabs are stopped. Let's see who cracks first.

Also today I went to the Media Workshops in Newcastle where some lads from South Shields, Richie Whitfield and Phil Turner, are setting up an exhibition that links together a local miners' strike in 1832, the General Strike of 1926, and the present dispute. They want to show how little has changed in the way the ruling class operate. It's an interesting fact that in 1832 William Jobling, a striking miner, was publicly gibbeted for allegedly murdering a local magistrate, the last person to suffer this terrible fate in Britain. It was a blatant attempt to break a strike organised by the newly formed union in the Durham coalfield, an attempt to scare men back to work. All that has changed today is that we can't be hung, yet, but Leon Brittan's threat of 'life sentences' for miners amounts to the same thing. Like the men in 1832, we won't be scared off!

Thursday October 4th, 1984

As expected, the jelly backs in NACODs have gone into talks with the NCB through ACAS. It's a bloody tragedy! After recording a strike vote that surprised us all the bastards have backed down. They could have done what we've so far failed to do, make Thatcher do another U-turn, and stop the scabs in Notts and elsewhere. I hope I'm wrong but I think they'll reach a compromise.

Gary, Keith and me had a meeting this afternoon at Gary's house. It was a useful exercise and one we hope to repeat on a weekly basis. The most important thing to come out of the meeting is our decision to re open the soup kitchen at Harton which closed during the summer due to lack of funds and lack of customers. Our first task is to start building up a reserve of cash to ensure we can keep it running once we start. We think it will be excellent because it can serve as a focal point for the strikers and a place where everyone can discuss their problems. At least it will give me something constructive to do.

Today is the 10th birthday of my youngest daughter, Sasha, and thanks to Kath's final pay packet we were able to give her a nice present, which is more than most strikers' kids will get. We have been lucky and it's a pity Kath can't appreciate that.

Saturday October 6th, 1984

The exhibition about the miners' strike put together by Richie Whitfield and Phil Turner opened in the Old Town Hall, South Shields, today and it is excellent. As well as a lot of old photographs and written material, the 'Coal Not Dole' videos are run constantly. We sold 22 papers and collected over £25 for the soup kitchen, which is brilliant. Most people who came today gave favourable comments, though one man said it was too one sided because there were no photos of pickets beating up police. Astonishing.

Whilst I was at the exhibition I had the chance to talk with members of the

Westoe Miners Wives Support Group and told them of our plans to reopen the soup kitchen. They wished us luck but said they were too busy dishing out food tokens to help. Fair enough. Hopefully we'll have enough money to start by the end of the month, just in time to meet 'General Winter'.

Wednesday October 10th, 1984

We had a union meeting this morning which showed the extent of the members' dissatisfaction with our Lodge officials. We had to elect a member to sit on the Durham Area Executive Committee, a post traditionally filled by one of the senior officials. Accordingly both the Chairman and the Treasurer were nominated by members of the committee. A rank and file member, Ed Malcolm, was nominated from the floor, and even though he is a soft left careerist I voted for him along with the majority on the floor. The result was absolutely brilliant. The Chairman got 15 votes, the Treasurer 6 votes, and Ed Malcolm got 54 votes! The lads were elated by this success, with most of us really enjoying the looks of utter shock on the stage. It was excellent, and a picket stood up to explain to the platform exactly why they had been given this vote of no confidence. The fact that they never appeared on picket lines, Tommy Wilson excepted, was given as the main reason, with the picket saying that you can't lead from a comfortable office! Man after man stood up to attack them, ending with a motion proposing that every picket of Westoe men must be attended by two officials, and that their places in the office should be filled by men banned from picketing. The Chairman got up and made a personal attack on me, full of vitriol, probably because I was the only man he knew who was banned from all picket lines, and because he thought, wrongly, that I was behind the attacks. He refused to accept the motion, saying he would have to ask his fellow committee men if they wanted to go on picket lines! At this all hell broke loose and without hesitation the bastard closed the meeting, and they all walked off the stage in a huff. We all complained loudly and bitterly, shouting for them to return, but they didn't. The lads were furious, but also jubilant at getting Ed elected.

The whole meeting was a perfect example of bureaucracy at work but at least the men now know, again, where the real power lies. Brilliant, and we must build on it at the next meeting and censure the Chairman for his undemocratic conduct.

The NUM have been fined £200,000 for refusing to comply with the Tory courts, and Scargill has been fined £1,000 for contempt. He has said that neither fine will be paid. Good for him.

Friday October 12th, 1984

Someone, probably the IRA, blew up the Grand Hotel in Brighton today but they missed Thatcher! Tebbit is reportedly badly injured but the rest of them got away.

No one has blamed violent pickets for it yet but no doubt they'll get round to it.

Most of the pickets I've spoken to are as jubilant as if we've won the strike. Of course, blowing up the bastards isn't the answer but at least it shows it's not just us miners who hate Thatcher and everything she stands for. They brought it upon themselves.

I spoke at Newcastle University and got a great reception. More importantly, they've promised to help us raise funds for the soup kitchen.

Wednesday October 17th, 1984

I travelled up to Newcastle with two women from the Wives Support Group, Alison and Marion. We'd been invited to attend a meeting at Newcastle Poly because the Tory students were going to try and reverse the decision to support the miners made at the start of the strike. During the course of the meeting, when Alison was nervously speaking and asking for support for the children, one of the Tories stood up and shouted,' If you want money why don't you send your husband back to work?' I just saw him disappear under a load of students keen to show him the error of his ways. He was lucky because if I'd had a chance to get at him I would have put up a much stronger argument! Anyway, the good news is the Tories were well defeated so the support stays. We got £17 from a collection. We also paid a visit to Newcastle and were given another £125. Alison and Marion were well chuffed.

The kitchen will now open next Monday at Harton Miners Welfare because we also received two cheques from comrades in Manchester SWP for £110. Their support throughout the strike has been magnificent and they've played a key role in establishing the credibility of the SWP at Westoe.

NACODs have called a strike to start on the 25th after talks with the NCB broke down. If they really mean it why not call the strike for tomorrow? I think it's so they can give the NCB time to buy them off. We'll see.

Saturday October 20th, 1984

Scargill addressed a big support rally in Sunderland this morning and survived an 'assassination' attempt from a crazy old woman armed with a tin of cat food. After interrogation by the police it has been disclosed that she has no connection to the strike whatsoever and her only motive was a dislike of dear old Arthur, and a liking for seeing herself on telly.

The rally itself was the usual affair, quite well attended but not by the people who needed to be there, the thousands sitting on their arses at home. If we can't get the message across to those men that passivity doesn't win strikes, then they are all potential scabs, and that could mean defeat. Scargill and cohorts should be speaking every day in every mining community instead of wasting their time in pointless negotiations.

Received yet another cheque for £60 from Manchester comrades. Fantastic.

Sunday October 21st, 1984

There was a union meeting this morning, called at short notice. I only found out because Gary called me early. We should have been prepared for a move like this because it was obvious they weren't going to let us build on the anger of the men at the last meeting. The Chairman proudly announced that two committee men have volunteered to attend picket lines, and he also announced that men banned from picket lines would be paid £2 a day if they helped the Women's Support Group. Unfortunately there weren't enough men present to mount an attack on the Chairman for his behaviour at the last meeting so he got away with it, this time. We should have campaigned more amongst the pickets, Still, we didn't so that's that.

Gary and I spent all afternoon and most of this evening cleaning out the Welfare, especially the kitchen, which is now spotless and ready to go, as is the 'Baby Burco' boiler which has been thoroughly scrubbed. We peeled the potatoes and carrots ready for tomorrow and left them in water overnight, as we did with the lentils and peas. Gary is a real fusspot and had us scrubbing every inch of the walls and floor but the end result was worth all the sweat. The Welfare has never looked so clean for months. All we need now is for a lot of people to use it.

Monday October 22nd, 1984

The kitchen got off to a great start as far as customers were concerned with about 80 pickets turning up. Unfortunately we had a bit of a disaster because all the lentils and peas stuck to the bottom of the boiler and burned the soup. We had to pour the lot down the drain. Fortunately we had plenty of bread and eggs so the lads didn't starve. An important lesson learnt, you must stir soup regularly!

A group of students from Newcastle Poly came down and gave us a cheque for £116 which they had collected over the weekend. This gave us a tremendous boost and we put a huge sheet of paper on the wall so that we can write down all the donations we receive and the pickets can clearly see who is supporting us. It will also put all finances into the open so we can hopefully avoid being accused of benefiting personally.

Some berk called Michael Eaton has been appointed as NCB spokesman to take over public announcements from Ian 'The Elephant Man' MacGregor who has become an embarrassment to his paymasters.

Wednesday October 24th, 1984

Oh gosh, what a surprise, NACODs have called off their threatened strike. Traitorous shitbags!

A coach load of our men were prevented from attending a 'No Sell Out' demonstration in Sheffield by the pigs. They were ordered to turn around and return to Durham. Oh gosh, what a surprise, who would have thought it?

As a result the soup kitchen was quiet today, unlike yesterday when we had a meeting with the Wives Support Group. They have changed their minds and are now totally against the kitchen, even though Gary and me are prepared to run it ourselves. They also took offence when we suggested they should be more open about their finances to prevent criticism. We tried to be constructive but got nowhere and they left. This doesn't bode well for the future if we can't work together. One positive thing is that Marion and Alison want to help because they are bored with just giving out food tokens. Gary and me went with them to the Trustees Saving Bank on Boldon Lane and we've opened an account in the name of 'Westoe Miners Soup Kitchen', casting originality to the wind. I am Secretary, Gary is the Chairman, Marion is Treasurer, and Alison is Assistant Secretary. We have £230 to start us off which should keep us going for a few weeks.

Today Marion and Alison brought along Florrie, who must be in her sixties, and is the most fantastic worker I've ever met. She looks frail but she works harder than anyone else and puts Gary and me to shame. She told me a great story about the 1972 strike. Her husband and two sons, Norman and John, worked at Westoe, and when she was out shopping one day in the local shop a woman made a nasty comment about miners. Florrie told her to watch her mouth and warned her not to repeat her remarks or she would stick her in the freezer! Foolishly the woman repeater her insults and Florrie carried out her threat and upended the woman straight into the chest freezer. The woman ran home to fetch her husband, and when he arrived Florrie said she'd do the same to him if he didn't shut up! They stormed out of the shop. I mention this story to show the wonderful spirit and pride of a fantastic woman, staunch in her support of the miners. She is an inspiration to us all and she typifies the fighting spirit of the mining communities.

Thursday October 25th, 1984

The bastards have stolen NUM funds because we refused to pay their unjust fine of £200,000 for contempt! Contempt is all I have for them! Surely now we'll get the support promised at Brighton from the rest of the unions? If they let the Tories get away with this, then they're allowing the same fate for themselves in the future, and that will be disastrous for the whole of the working class. The NACODs leadership must be really thick if they can't see the significance of the timing of this attack, straight after their sell out. The sooner they realise that they've won no concessions at all the sooner we can begin the long overdue attack on Thatcher's plans to decimate the mining industry and the NUM as a fighting union!

I spoke to the Newcastle University Miners Support Group about what we are attempting to do with the kitchen and the financial support we need. They've promised to do what they can, which is all we can ask for.

More people are starting to use the kitchen, which is very encouraging. The word is starting to spread about what we are trying to do, especially today when people came to the kitchen to collect their £2 food tokens and saw at first hand what is going on. A lot of them expressed approval about the notice on the wall showing donations, which is gratifying because some of the Wives Support Group said it was a bad idea. We also make all our account books available on a table so people can see exactly how the money is being spent. People are beginning to ask why the WSG can't do the same, which has really pissed them off. They've accused us of causing problems but they should realise there are a lot of vicious rumours circulating about them which does nothing for morale.

Friday October 26th, 1984

We had a very busy day in the kitchen, serving over 100 bowls of broth, which is a vast improvement on Monday's poor start. Gary takes the credit for this. He's a dab hand in the kitchen and seems to really enjoy the cooking. He won't let anyone near 'his broth', except to give it the occasional stir. This is fine by me because I much prefer fundraising.

We received yet another cheque from Manchester for £49 which is a welcome addition to our funds. We also received a visit from a couple of journalists from the local evening rag, not renowned for its support of the strike, or miners in general. I wasn't too surprised because one of them is a comrade, which just goes to show the SWP attracts all sections of the workforce. They gave us a cheque for £16 which we gratefully received. It's even more important because we can add the NUJ to our list of supporters and this will give a boost to people who are beginning to feel that everyone is against them.

Tuesday October 30th, 1984

Gary and I attended a meeting in Gateshead organised by the NALGO Support Group. It was a very constructive meeting, though we had some tricky questions to answer about Scargill and his alleged visit to Libya, as revealed by the *Sunday*

Times. All we could think of to reply was the fact that because the Tories are trying to starve us back to work then we have the right to accept money from wherever we can get it from. We also said that the Tories themselves have bought oil and other goods from Libya so they were hypocrites. Anyway, we have been promised support and that's the important thing.

Privately I think Scargill has made a stupid mistake in giving the Tories and their media even more ammunition in their campaign to totally discredit him. He should've sent someone who couldn't be linked to the NUM. That's what the Tories do.

The situation between Kath and myself is growing worse. We can't even talk to each other and she is still very bitter about losing her job. She blames me for it because of being active and getting arrested. Things can't go on like this because the strike gives me enough hassle without her adding to it.

Saturday November 3rd, 1984

Even the bloody weather was against us today, with pouring rain spoiling the firework display we had organised for the kids outside the kitchen. It didn't dampen our spirits though and it was a great success. Bob Delbridge and some other students at Newcastle Poly had made two brilliant effigies of Thatcher and MacGregor which sat on top of the bonfire, with a full outline of the Houses of Parliament placed in front. When the black paper burned away it revealed the slogan 'Victory to the Miners', complete with SWP fist, and the crowd cheered. There were a few hundred people present to watch the spectacle, braving the rain, and applauding loudly when Thatcher and MacGregor burned. It's just a pity we didn't have the real thing!

We provided hot food and drinks in the kitchen and were rushed off our feet keeping up with demand. The children had a great time, which was the whole point, and they loved the bonfire and fireworks. It's a shame we couldn't have gotten hold of the recently departed Mrs Gandhi, then we could have burned three bastards instead of two!

Monday November 5th, 1984

Well, the strain has finally caught up with Kath and she has suggested that we split up. I didn't argue because home life has become unbearable and it was starting to affect the girls. We've agreed that a separation would be best for all of us and I will leave as soon as I can find somewhere to stay. 12 years down the pan! Thank you, Thatcher! Perhaps when the strike is finally over we can get back together though I doubt it because there is no way I am ever going back down the pit again. I've been saying it for months, win or lose, and I can't really see Kath wanting to be with me when I'm unemployed. Que sera sera.

Chris Moore phoned to say the Redskins are playing the Bunker Club in Sunderland tomorrow night and has invited Kath and me along. Kath doesn't want to go so I'll go on my own. I need something to cheer me up.

Kinnock has refused to attend a series of planned rallies. Just proves where his true loyalties lie.

The Delegate Conference has voted unanimously to continue the strike, which is heartening in the light of concerted efforts by the NCB to bribe men back to work. The bastards are trying hard to get NUM funds but they aren't finding it easy. Let's hope it stays that way.

Tuesday November 6th, 1984

I really enjoyed the Redskins' gig tonight at the Bunker Club, a miner's benefit, and the band were brilliant. They played with passion and the lyrics are excellent. I loved the music as well, great brass section. My favourite was 'Keep on Keepin' On', because I could really relate to the line, 'I'm not down but I'm feeling low'. Kind of sums me up just now. Mind you, I did feel a little out of place amongst the fashionable Sunderland crowd.

Afterwards Chris told me the band are appearing on live TV on Friday, on *The Tube* and asked me if I would make a brief appearance. I didn't need to be asked twice and I'm visiting them for rehearsals on Thursday in Newcastle. I'm excited!

Thursday November 8th, 1984

I spent the morning helping out in the kitchen, then headed off up to Newcastle, to meet the Redskins in the Tyne Tees Television studios on City Road. I watched the band rehearse, then we got together to plan what I would say tomorrow. Chris reckons it'll only take about 20 to 30 seconds for them to work out what is happening so we worked on what I could say in that time. I was thrilled to meet Rik Mayall because I loved the *Young Ones* but I was a bit disappointed that he speaks quite posh and not like his character. Daft, I suppose, but there you go.

This evening we went for a lovely Chinese meal in Newcastle and I got to know Martin and Nick a bit better, and Adrian, the band's manager. Chris said that I'm welcome to spend some time at his flat in London after I told him Kath and I have split up. I think that's what I'll do because it will get me away from Kath, and I can perhaps do some fundraising when I'm there. Xmas is only a month away and we need to give the kids a good time if we can. I really enjoyed myself.

I spent the night on a friend's couch in Newcastle, one of the students from the Poly.

Friday November 9th, 1984

What a great experience, and a very controversial one! I arrived at the studio and was given an 'artistes' badge for security by Adrian Collins, the Redskins manager. I was really, really nervous, and rehearsed my speech in the toilets to try and get it word perfect. I kept a low profile as the studio began to fill up with the audience. I was really surprised at how small it is because on the telly it looks huge. I watched The Alarm and Billy Bragg before joining the band for their bit. I was to stand at the back between the drums and the brass section, clutching a tambourine for the first song, 'Hold On', then come out for my bit after being introduced by Chris.

I was literally shaking with fear as the song closed and the lights went off briefly as Nick played the drum intro. Chris spoke into his mike and introduced me by saying, 'On extra percussion, tambourine, and on strike for 35 weeks, a Durham miner', at which point I stepped forward to the mike. I can't honestly remember speaking, I only noticed the audience applauding loudly when I'd finished. Then I walked to the back of the stage as Chris sang the song 'Keep On Keepin' On'.*

As soon as the band finished we all headed backstage to the 'green' room to recover. It wasn't green but Martin told me that's what they call the place where you get free drinks and within seconds I'd downed a pint of lager. Billy Bragg came over and said no one had heard a word of my speech. I was really disappointed because all that worry and nerves had been for nothing. I got a triple Southern Comfort with ice but was called outside to see Jools Holland and he said that if I'd told them what I was going to do they would've made sure I was heard. A load of bollocks! Loads of people spoke to me and expressed their support for the strike, including *The Tube's* press officer, who wanted to know what I'd said so I told them.

> "There's been six miners killed in this strike, five miners on life support machines, three miners with fractured skulls, over 2,500 serious injuries and more than 7,500 arrests. We're told we're out on a limb, we're on our own, and that no one supports us, yet hundreds of thousands of pounds have been collected for us by working class people – miners support groups have sprung up all over the country in towns, factories, offices and colleges. They're supporting us – you should be supporting them!"

Anyway, I got pissed on free booze, met the stars and enjoyed the rest of the show.

---

*You can watch my appearance on *The Tube* at
http://www.youtube.com/watch?v=RVMVbBmj7MM&feature=related

I travelled down to London in the van with the roadies and am now comfortably settled on Chris's settee in his flat in Willesden Green. At Cortonwood there has been an invasion of over 1,000 pigs to get one scab into work. Anyone who can try to justify that needs their head looking at. Majority rules and the majority are still on strike, ballot or no fuckin' ballot. That's a fact.

Monday November 12th, 1984

Today is Jennifer's 12th birthday and it's the first one I've not been there for her. I spoke to her on the phone and promised to bring her a present when I get home, but it's not the same and I felt really depressed today. Sorry, sweetheart, I really am.

Chris took me along to his record company, London Records, so that the band's press officer, Eugene, could put together a press release about *The Tube*. It was a novel experience for me and I was surprised they could get a photo from the TV to use with it. Best of all, I was allowed to help myself to as many records as I could carry. I got a pile of old Rolling Stones stuff, and some records I thought the girls might like, The Fine Young Cannibals and others. I think Chris was a bit embarrassed as we left with me struggling to carry my booty. It was excellent!

This afternoon a London comrade took me to a DHSS office in Harrow and the workers there have agreed to support the soup kitchen, which is brilliant.

Norman Willis, the new fat bastard in charge of the TUC, spoke at a miners' rally in Wales and had the bloody nerve to condemn picket line violence! What planet are these people on? The miners responded by booing loudly until some enterprising lads lowered a noose in front of him. They should've bloody lynched him! I thought Len Murray was a disgrace but this man makes him seem militant.

The NCB have offered a £650 Christmas bonus to anyone who scabs before November ends. Bastards!

Friday November 16th, 1984

I have spent the week visiting colleges and factories from Kilburn to Croydon but the best meeting happened this morning at the Central Middlesex Hospital, near Neasden. I had been invited to speak by the NALGO shop stewards and my audience was a group of female office workers who I was warned were very hostile to the strike. They stopped work and listened to me for about ten minutes as I told them about my own experience of the strike, and how I saw picket line violence, about being jailed and banned off picket lines, and how I was trying to collect funds for the kitchen. I told them how the families of striking miners got next to nothing off the state, and single miners got nothing at all. They fired all the usual questions at me, ie why should taxpayers keep uneconomic pits open. I asked them how much they thought the electricity bills would go up if we end up relying on foreign coal? I felt really good when we'd finished, with them agreeing to pay a weekly levy to the Westoe kitchen. Not only that but a woman who had asked the hardest questions gave me a fiver from her purse. This has shown me yet again that even the most hardened of critics can have their views changed by hearing our side of the story.

The Redskins have gone on tour but Chris has let me stay until he gets back. Kath hasn't returned my calls so I guess our marriage really is over. Can't take it in somehow. Unreal.

Bloody hell! Just had a phone call telling me 30 scabs have gone into Westoe, straight through the picket line in a 'battlebus', all silvered windows and steel mesh. I can't believe it, though they reckon most of them are from affiliated unions, not the NUM. How do they know? As far as I'm concerned the union officials at Westoe are responsible for this because they did nothing to get men on the picket lines, even after the disgraceful attack on the community by the pigs. We must get to these passive men somehow because if we don't 30 will turn into 300!

I did a paper sale at Dollis Hill tube and was shown the site of Grunwick's. It's a pity we can't get the same support! Sold 5 papers and got almost £10 in a bucket collection.

Monday November 19th, 1984

I was invited to an SWP Cocktail Party last night, in Harlesden, I think. It was hosted in the home of Steve and Fiona Brown, a lovely couple, but those bloody cocktail things are friggin' lethal! I passed out well before the end and woke in the early hours and staggered back to Chris's. It was all in a good cause because they raised £66, and Steve and Fiona added £50 from their own pockets. I phoned Marion at the kitchen and she told me they urgently need funds because they are now dealing with 250 pickets a day plus a lot of families. Just makes me wonder what would have happened at lots of places if they'd joined us a lot earlier. It's just a pity its taken scabs at the pit to get them off their arses! I sent off all the money I'd collected so far and sent it off registered post. They should get it tomorrow.

Tuesday November 20th, 1984

I visited bus depots in Cricklewood, Westbourne Park, and Shepherds Bush. I managed to get the mechanics at one garage twinned with the kitchen but everyone else was already committed elsewhere. I did a first for me, addressing a meeting on the top deck of a bus because management wouldn't allow me in the depot. It was a novel experience and fairly successful. No money but good support. One thing I noticed today was the tremendous support we get from the black community. I know what Brixton was really about now having been at the 'Battle of Orgreave', and am a proud card carrying member of the 'Enemy Within'.

Friday November 23rd, 1984
II heard from my solicitor in Newcastle this morning that my trial in Edinburgh has been set for February 7th, no bail conditions. Civilised people, the Scots. Me mam always calls them 'Scotchies'.

Gary rang and told me only 7 scabs had gone into Westoe this morning because they'd been visited and shown the error of their ways! Good! Mind you, the NCB have offered another bribe of £175 plus back pay to any miner who returns to work before next Friday. The bastards are getting really desperate now, but their 30 pieces of silver will only succeed with a tiny minority.

The majority of us will treat it with the contempt it deserves, especially as it comes straight after the Tories deducting a further £1 from the pittance a miner's family is supposed to live on, about £14 a week, all normal bills expected to be paid. Debt! Single miners get nothing, not even picket pay for me just now, charity case living off handouts from supporters.

I met some ambulance drivers in Kenton and was given £20 in cash, and the promise of regular sums to be sent to the kitchen. If all this money from London is written on the sheet at Westoe it should really give them heart to see the range of their support.

I can speak to Jen and Sasha but Kath just refuses to speak to me. Bloody hell, I just don't think I deserve this.

Wednesday November 28th, 1984
Adrian, the Redskins manager, 'hired' me as a 'roadie' for their gig in Hammersmith Town Hall but it was really a gesture of solidarity because there was no work for me to do. A man has to live.

It was a brilliant gig and the band were on top form in front of 1,200 fans. I was really embarrassed by the number of people who recognised me from *The Tube* but it did give me a chance to have some good discussions, and my collection bucket was really full. The Three Johns were the support band and I really loved their set. Jon Langford is a brilliant guitarist and the guy on vocals is manic. Excellent. I got the chance to speak in front of my biggest audience yet and got a fantastic reception. Good for the ego.

After the gig I collected with some Kent miners and when we counted it up we found we had £210, which was brilliant. Chris told us there were some striking miners from Notts who were worse off than us so I halved my share with them because the Kent miners refused point blank to give them anything. They disgusted me to be honest because there are fewer miners in Kent than at Westoe alone, and they have really milked the support from London. So much for solidarity!

Thursday November 29th, 1984
I did a strange interview with a journalist called 'Tiny' for a glossy magazine called *Debut*. God knows how it will look when it comes out, if it ever does.

Friday November 30th,
Got a lift down to Brighton with Debbie and Sue, band girlfriends, to see The Redskins perform again. They were shit hot, really tight, and the brass section was blasting out all the songs I'm growing to love, 'Keep On Keepin' On', 'Go Get Organised', 'Take No Heroes', '16 Tons'. Great stuff! Martin called for me to go on stage and I was bloody blushing because the packed crowd were chanting, 'We want Norman Strike, we want Norman Strike'. I felt like a pop star myself! I made a speech and got a tremendous round of applause. Wish I could do this every night, especially the free food and booze in the dressing room afterwards! Early hours car ride back to London, flying.

Sunday December 2nd, 1984
I attended the National Miners Support Group Conference in Camden Town Hall. It was so well attended that over 1,400 people turned up, and an overflow meeting had to be set up in the nearby University of London for 500 people. Tony Benn said nothing but spoke for 15 minutes, and Scargill never even turned up. I was asked to speak at the overflow meeting and did. Got a good reception. Encouraging to see so much support and more money for the soup kitchen, £101, from the bucket.

Thursday December 6th, 1984
I've been very homesick for the past few days so I decided to go home to see Kath and the girls on impulse. I caught the Newcastle coach from St.Pancras and arrived on my doorstep at around three. Kath opened the door with the words, 'What the hell are you doing here?' and it went downhill from there. I've spent the whole night talking to her, or at her would be closer to the truth. She just ignored me and seemed really bitter I'm here. I'm off back down to London first thing. Stuff her. At least I tried. The girls don't understand what's going on and it's not bloody fair. Selfish cow.

Friday December 7th, 1984
I left a short note on the kitchen table and left really early while they were all sleeping. The bloody couch was bloody uncomfortable, and cold. Not as cold as her bloody bed!
    Back on the couch in Chris's front room, which is comfortable.

Wednesday December 12th, 1984

I've spent the last couple of days in Croydon as a guest of Steve, an SWP comrade. He has been great, helping me to raise yet more funds for the kitchen. The best was this evening when I spoke to a large group of shop stewards at a factory in East Croydon. They weren't an easy audience and asked a lot of hard questions, especially about the death of a Welsh taxi driver taking a scab to work. My answer to that is that if we had been allowed to picket then men wouldn't have been forced into such desperate actions away from the pit. My only regret is that the scab survived! I received good applause and a promise of financial support for the kitchen.

Kath rang tonight to apologise for her cold reception of last week and asked me to return to spend Christmas as a family. I said yes and am going back on Friday. I have to go back anyway for my court appearance though I'm expecting to stay at Paul McGarr's place in Newcastle and visit home during the day. We'll have to see how it goes.

Friday December 14th, 1984

Last night I went to the London Records Xmas party and got totally and utterly pissed. I probably made a complete fool of myself. I do remember having a row with a radio DJ about the strike and calling him an arsehole, and leering at Bananarama. I must have been pissed! I found a straw boater on the floor when I came round this morning and I vaguely remember someone saying it belonged to Elton John, but he wasn't there. Perhaps I can raffle it to raise funds?

I caught the train home from King's Cross, ticket paid for by Chris. My welcome home was a huge improvement on the last time, and I'm beginning to hope we can sort out our problems.

We went out together tonight and spent most of it talking about the future and whether the strike will go on much longer. I told her it has a long way to go yet. The only good thing about our split is that her and the girls are living much better because they are getting proper support from the DHSS, such as it is. We'll see what happens.

Monday December 17th, 1984

Today we had our Xmas Dinner in the kitchen and it was brilliant! The place was packed with families and single lads and we had entertainment, live music and a three course dinner with turkey and stuffing. There were also presents for the kids given personally by Santa but provided by all our supporters. I felt really proud at how things have grown since our small start, all thanks to the hard work of Gary, Florrie, Marion, Alison, Maureen and George, and the support from the long list of donors on sheets of paper hanging on the walls. We have achieved what we set out to do and that was to provide a focal point where people can come and sit in the warm and share their hopes and fears, and have a really nice meal. Jen and Sasha love it here, though Kath never brings them, probably to avoid questions about me.

Strangely I felt a bit like an outsider until Gary told me to come back down to earth and get back to being a poverty stricken miner instead of hobnobbing amongst the stars. He is right, but it was a good experience, even if it does make me feel guilty. Nowt new there then.

JUSTICE

Tuesday December 18th, 1984
I finally appeared at Sunderland Magistrates Court this afternoon and won! All those months of being banned from picketing, not to mention 3 days in jail, and the case is thrown out because the pigs cocked it up big time!

I was waiting outside of the courtroom with my two witnesses, Ian and Mick, and the cop who'd been photographed with me, but who hadn't arrested me, didn't seem to recognise who I was.

I was called in to see my barrister and she asked me if I had any information which could help my case. I stressed that I had been arrested by two officers, an Inspector and a Sergeant, and the young PC credited with my arrest had actually been sitting in the van I had been thrown into after being dragged there by the officers. I also said he was sitting outside and I got the feeling he didn't know who I was. A man got up and left the room. My Barrister, a very clever woman, told me the police had offered to reduce the charge if I would plead guilty. I refused on principle, but also because I gave her a very clear photograph of the two officers dragging me towards the van.

Inside the courtroom I was very nervous and sat facing the bench. On the right there was a diagram of the alleged crime scene at Wearmouth. The young PC was called as the first and only witness for the prosecution, and was asked if he could identify the defendant in court. What a bloody joke! Of course he could bloody recognise me because I was sitting where defendants bloody sit! He then gave his version of what happened on the morning of September 5th 1984, using the diagram to illustrate his points. According to him I had been at the head of a large body of pickets, lashing out at the police with feet and fists and behaving like a violent thug. He said that I had viciously attacked an Inspector, knocking him to the ground before leaping on him and grabbing him round the throat, trying to throttle him. The young PC then arrested me by shoving my right arm up my back and leading me to the van and being put inside. When he'd finished the Magistrate looked as if he was just about to have me hung, I was totally stunned.

My Barrister went straight onto the attack and asked if the 'assaulted' Inspector was in the court? He wasn't. She then asked for his name, and the young PC nervously admitted that he didn't know. She began to pour scorn on his evidence, suggesting that if his statement were to be believed, I had seriously assaulted a senior police officer who was not in court and couldn't be named. Surely the charge should be serious assault, if not attempted murder, not just 'Breach of the Peace'. The young PC was gobsmacked and was unable to explain any of it.

The Barrister then went for the throat and said, 'I would remind you, officer, that you are on oath and that perjury is a very serious crime.' She then asked him if it was not true that when a colleague of hers asked the PC, just before the court started, 'Have you seen Norman Strike, its urgent?' you replied, 'I wouldn't know him if I saw him.' The PC stuttered that he hadn't said that exactly, but she cut him short by reminding him again that he was still on oath. He then admitted that he had said that but added that I was definitely the man he arrested because he recognised my face! She said that he could have seen me lots of times on previous days and he had to admit that was possible. She told the Magistrate that there was insufficient evidence to prove the charge against me and that it should be dropped. The Magistrate did some whispering and then, reluctantly it seemed to me, dismissed the case. Brilliant!

I thanked the Barrister and young man for their help and asked if there was any chance of me suing the police for wrongful arrest and imprisonment. She advised me to be content with my escape and not to push the police too far. It wouldn't be a good move.

As I was being congratulated by Mick and Ian, the Young PC wished me and my family a very merry Xmas, and added he was glad I got off! I couldn't believe my ears. If he'd been believed I might have been spending Xmas behind bars! Then he accused my lawyer of using dirty tricks to trap him! I wanted to punch him but didn't want any more grief so I just thanked him for confirming that the pigs are liars and cannot be trusted, and walked off with the lads to celebrate.

Justice 1984!

Thursday December 20th, 1984

My luck is changing! A comrade who works in the DHSS rang me to tell me about a special grant being paid to single miners living in Newcastle, £126. Because I've been staying in Benwell, off and on, since November I qualified for the payment and went and got it, no problems at all. I spent the afternoon blowing every penny on buying presents for Kath and the girls. Stuff the future, and it was worth it to see the look on Kath's face when I got back. At least Xmas hasn't been cancelled this year for the girls. They are what this fight is all about and their happiness comes above all else, to me at least.

1980 FUCKIN' 5

Tuesday January 1st, 1985
As today is the first of a New Year, 1985, and we are still on strike, it seems a good time to try and look back at 1984, the most exciting, frightening and educational year of my life so far, and also one of the saddest. I never imagined it would last this long, and still be going strong.

1984 began with a foretaste of what was to come when two hundred of us were sent home by management on January 3rd at 3.30am. This was because of the national overtime ban and the way the colliery winder men, six of them, chose to operate it. They refused to start work until 7am, and because they are the men responsible for getting men down the pit, we were sent home, losing a days pay into the bargain. The winder men are an elite, and on good money because of the overtime they got. They were against the overtime ban and showed their dissatisfaction by costing us a day's pay as revenge. Stupid bastards couldn't see any further than pay day. Naturally this caused a lot of anger and resentment, and the militancy of the strike we had towards the end of 1983 began to grow. Our Incentive payments were no incentive at all, a pittance, and always have been. Not for us the new cars and holidays and bloody caravans of the men in the easy seams in the Midlands. Ours are hard to get at, and very wet due to us working under the North Sea. The harder you work the less you get. We are miles behind the 'two hundred quid a week miners' the media bleat about if we dare to ask for a pay rise. This dispute was soon resolved but really wound up the lads, especially the younger lads who were beginning to listen to what Scargill was telling them. They know Westoe loses money because of lack of proper investment, and if the grounds for closing a pit is to be uneconomic, then we were in the front ranks. That's why the strike vote was so emphatic, and here I am, here we are, here we go.

There have been a lot of positives from the struggle, most notably the women who have been the backbone of the strike, not only working in the soup kitchens but also going out and speaking to conferences and meetings, and speaking out in the media. They've been on picket lines and suffered the police violence in their own communities, eyes opened never to close again. Most of the women say things will never go back to the way they were and they are determined to stick together to help others once the strike is eventually won. Good on them.

Another thing is the way thousands of striking miners and their families have no illusions about the police and where their loyalties really lie, for the bosses and against the workers. Before the strike I would say a lot of miners believed most of what they read in the papers or saw on the telly, but now, through personal experience, they have learnt to question and be critical. They used to respect the police and now they despise them. We've seen them at their work, really enjoying it as they beat the shit out of men, women and kids, no mercy. The Special Patrol Group, Direct Response Unit, are forces everyone should be concerned about. It's us today but who will it be tomorrow? They are highly trained thugs that even the 'ordinary' police hold in fear. I've heard 'ordinary' pigs call them 'animals', and 'psychopaths'. The relationship between the police and the mining communities has been irreparably damaged and can never get back to what it was.

Of course the key factor in this strike has been the mass scabbing of men in Notts and the Midlands, and when I hear the bastards say shit like they would have been with us on the line if they'd been allowed a national ballot I get really angry. And how can they bear to be praised by Thatcher! She'll stab them in the back one day and close their pits. I hope fuckin' 'Silver Birch' gets terminal cancer and dies a painful death, traitorous scum. He's the real 'enemy within'!

I hate the scabs who've gone back in the past few months because they have really sold us out after being on our side, taking their poxy silver. They give pathetic excuses about poverty and debt but don't realise that they will be in worse poverty and debt if the pit closes. We won't always be on strike but they'll always be scabs!

From a personal point of view 1984 has changed my life completely, from being a mostly unambitious, stuck in a deep rut miner, to a confident, want something better from life revolutionary socialist. I must also be slightly mad because I'm fighting for a job I don't want. I'm not sure what I do want but am certain it includes daylight and fresh, clean air. I would wish Kath and me stick with each other but it isn't looking good. Let's win the strike first.

Wednesday January 2nd, 1985

Today was my first back on a picket line since September. Then it was to stop 7 scabs at Wearmouth; now it's to stop the 56 scabs claimed by the NCB at my own pit, Westoe. Problem is, no attempt at all was made to stop any of the three buses that sped into the pit. The very fact they are using three buses when one would do shows the Board's desperation to convince men to scab, and the media keeps us constantly reminded that the scab numbers are rising. It's very discouraging. I seem to have been saying the same thing since the start of the strike but that doesn't make it less true. We need MASS PICKETS to push and shove against the pigs to stop the scabs. We could have had a go with the 200 men present today but no one was trying to organise or encourage.

If the depressing mood at Westoe is being repeated elsewhere then the strike is headed for a sell out at best, total defeat at worst. Shouting scab at faceless traitors won't stop them going into work, and neither will vandalising their homes, because the NCB just pays for repairs.

Friday January 4th, 1985

According to the NCB 72 scabs went into Westoe today, 3,177 in the North East Area. No difference on the picket line, passivity and resignation, doom and gloom. The end seems nigh.

This afternoon I decided to take Jen and Sasha down to the picket line because I knew there'd be no trouble, but just in case we stood away from the main body of pickets. I just wanted to explain what has been happening for almost a year, and to show them the scab buses and also explain what kind of people were hiding inside. I know that Sasha is only 10, and Jen is 12, but why shouldn't they know why their mam and dad have split up?

Predictably a television crew had turned up from Tyne Tees Television to film the 3 buses going in so that passive miners, who still have tellies, can see how quiet it is. Some of the lads jumped in front of the camera to ruin their filming as the scab buses went in, and one of the escort vans full of riot police stopped and they poured out ready for action, pushing into our lads and trying hard to get them to retaliate. The lads knew their tactics and didn't respond. I pointed this out to my daughters and told them never to forget what they were seeing, and hearing, in January 1985. Sasha said, 'They should push the police back. I would!' Out of the mouths of babes!

The pigs crawled back into their van and continued to mock the pickets, waving money at them. I again pointed this out to the girls and explained what they were doing before leading them off to return home. We had just turned the corner when a police van pulled up just ahead of us and an Inspector, two pips on his shoulder, leant out of the window and said, 'Hoy! You! What were you saying to those children?' Anger welled up inside me and I snapped back, 'What the hell has that got to do with you? They're my kids and our conversation is private!' His reply staggered me! 'I hope you weren't trying to warp their minds against the police.' I can't remember exactly what I said in reply but it was along the lines that things hadn't got so bad that I was forced to repeat conversations with my girls to the police. His response shocked even me, a hardened picket. 'I'll tell you what then, mate. When those kids', pointing at my terrified daughters, 'get fucking lost, or something fucking worse happens to them, don't phone for us, phone for fucking Arthur Scargill!' The van sped off and I was left trying to comfort my frightened kids. What the fuck have we come to that innocent little girls have to be scared witless because their dad is a striking miner?

Monday January 7th, 1985

The NCB are claiming over 1,000 men returned to work today. At Westoe, as at other pits in the North East, they were expecting a huge surge back. It never happened at Westoe, though there were a few more than Friday. There was a very discouraging return at Herrington, led by the Lodge Chairman, a rat called Joe Stokoe. Also, at Ellington, the Lodge Secretary led a return to work, despite his son being a leading member of *Militant*. These two dickheads claim an allegiance to the NUM, and will almost certainly encourage more scabbing from the so called 'moderate miners' who have sat on their arses for 10 months! Bastards!

The situation at Wearmouth just gets worse and I feel really sorry for their predominantly left wing officials because they have a lot more scabs than us, and our officials have been crap whilst theirs have been excellent. It just doesn't make sense.

Wednesday January 9th, 1985

The NCB are claiming 101 scabs at Westoe but we reckon there are only about 65. Guess which figures will be reported in the media? The picketing is depressing and frustrating. Even when two lads got lifted for refusing to move off the pavement no one retaliated. A few months ago at least we would have marched to the pig shop to complain. Today, a big fat nowt!

I resigned as Secretary of the soup kitchen because I'm pissed off with the infighting between two groups. Down, down, deeper and down.

Tonight I watched a programme on Channel 4 called, *Whose Side Are You On?* It was excellent, showing the magnificent spirit of the men and women to fight on against all adversity during the strike. The best thing though was the showing of police violence against us and our communities. However, the very showing of the programme means we have lost! At least that's what I think! How many people watch Ch4?

Thursday January 10th, 1985

A group of young striking miners have been sentenced to two and a half years in prison in Derbyshire for setting fire to scab buses. No one was hurt and I think the rest of the trade union movement should be ashamed of themselves for allowing it to happen. 'I'm not down but I'm feeling low.'

Monday January 14th, 1985
Since my last entry a Kent miner has been sentenced to 5 years in prison for allegedly stamping on a pig's face. How many years did the pigs get for beating the shit out of men at Orgreave and loads of other places? You know the answer!!

The tension between Kath and myself grows day by day, and we just aren't talking to each other again. I am really depressed and really can't see any point in carrying on. Thatcher has a lot to answer for, bitch!

Wednesday January 16th, 1985
At long last we have seen some vigour and determination on the picket line at Westoe. The mostly young lads had had enough and began a serious push against the pigs, taking them by surprise because they've grown used to our passivity. We didn't stop the scabs but we did get back some of the fighting spirit I thought was lost for ever.

The situation at Wearmouth grows worse by the day, with almost a quarter of the workforce, 500 men, now scabbing. This has really damaged morale because Wearmouth has always been the most militant pit. If scabbing is so bad there, then how long can the rest of us continue?

Thursday January 17th, 1985
Looking out of my bedroom window this morning gave the perfect start to the day. A blizzard was raging outside and the ground was covered in deep snow, a sight only a striking miner could appreciate.

My good mood quickly disappeared down at the picket line because everyone seemed content merely to shout at the scab buses, shattering my optimism of yesterday that a new mood of militancy was growing.

Scargill spoke in Durham today, desperately trying to raise the morale of his flagging troops, with over 3,000 lads present. Why didn't he tell them to march to one of the scabby pits, such as Wearmouth? A golden opportunity lost. According to him, power station workers in Yorkshire are on the verge of striking, so why wasn't he speaking to them? It's alright hitting the Tories in their pockets, but Scargill seems unable to realise they will spend what it takes to defeat us, and get their money back in the long run. When we are gone.

Also today, in the House of Commons, the 'Campaign' group of left wing MPs began to do what they should have done from day one. They demanded a debate in government time on the strike, and when that was denied, they caused a row and parliament was suspended. Dennis Skinner told Thatcher, 'You aint seen nothing yet!'

A large part of British Rail went on strike today in support of men sacked for supporting our strike. It's only a pity they hadn't done this a lot earlier and we might just have won!

To end on a high note, a scab has been seriously injured at Westoe and we can only hope the bastard dies in agony!

Friday January 18th, 1985

The snow has gone as quickly as it appeared! It's still bitterly cold and passive picketing is again the order of the day. The Lodge officials do nothing, seemingly content for it to reach its expected conclusion, defeat!

The NCB are claiming 135 back at work, but we reckon there are only 24 NUM members included in that number, with 45 mechanics and 35 COSA members. Still, it's enough for the bastards to encourage others to become scabs.

Kneel Kinnock spoke today and yet again showed his true colours, a whiter shade of white! He said of yesterday's protest of Skinner and co, 'If they think the miners are helped, or the Labour Party is helped by what they are doing, then they are not living in the real world.' Earth calling Kinnock on Mars!!!!! Bloody idiot. In complete contrast 500 rank and file labour activists joined picket lines in Yorkshire.

Monday January 21st, 1985

It was totally pissing down with rain this morning and I really wanted to stay in bed. I forced myself out of bed and down to the line because I still believe we can win despite the passivity of others. One lad, Tony Scott, was arrested by the pigs, and it was great to hear the 'Zulu' chant one more time.

The NCB have crowed louder than usual today, claiming 651 new men returning to work. The biggest scabbing happened at Ellington Colliery in Northumberland, where 147 men scabbed and brought the total to 600.

There are now 4,812 scabs in the North East, almost a quarter of the workforce, and it would be stupid if we were not concerned. David Archibald, Area Director, said on TV: 'These men returning reinforce our view that the collapse of the strike is inevitable and gets nearer as each week passes.'

The national picture is no better, with the NCB claiming 40% now scabbing. Thatcher is going for the jugular and is refusing to hold talks without a guaranteed sell out.

Thursday January 31st, 1984

I received a letter through the post from the Manager of Westoe Colliery appealing for me to return to work so that the pit can be saved. Apparently it is in danger of being flooded so badly we won't be able to save it if we don't return to work NOW. Bollocks, it's blackmail. They've tried bribery and that didn't work so now it's blackmail. The letter ends, 'Remember, it is YOUR JOB and YOUR FUTURE at stake and requires YOUR decision NOW!' The bin got my response.

The Lodge has asked for our Safety Rep to be allowed down the pit to assess the situation but the manager, predictably, refused. The fact of the matter is its not us he wants back, it's the Deputies in the NACODs union because without them they can't get the scabs back down the pit. NACODs have so far refused to cross our picket lines because they know they will have to work with us once the strike is over, but that doesn't mean anything to the NCB and they are really being put under pressure. I've no sympathy for the bastards at all because if they'd joined the strike at the start we would have won this bloody strike months ago!

As expected, the NCB have refused to talk to the NUM unless they agree not to oppose pit closures. How can they expect us to do that after all the shit we've been through? Bastards are just building up hopes and then crushing them in the hope more men will return to work. 5,000 scabs now in the North East.

Four scab buses went into Westoe this morning and three men were arrested in the push. The pigs just grab anyone they can catch. The NCB are claiming 185 men working at Westoe. They neglect to mention that 100 of these are in the COSA union, 53 mechanics and the remainder genuine NUM scabs. Hardly a massive return to work from a workforce of over 2,000 men! I'm proud of the Westoe pickets, and always will be!

Monday February 4th, 1985
I got up at 4am this morning so I could get down to Westoe for the mass picket called in response to Westoe NACODs voting for a return to work, but only if there wasn't a hostile picket at the gates. It was brilliant! Over 500 men turned out to face one senior pig, as requested by NACODs. We were very hostile as we marched to the pit gates with the 'Zulu chant' being shouted loudly. Just like the good old days. We spotted a man in a car beside the pit, and when we asked him who he was he told us he was a reporter from the *Shields Gazette*, notorious amongst the pickets for its pro-scab, pro-NCB stance. He was lucky to get away alive as we began to rock his car and almost turned his world upside down.

The Deputies' leader was very arrogant in his short discussion with our officials, resulting in a hail of paint bombs, stones and traffic bollards raining down on the Deputies, forcing them into a very undignified retreat. Things then started to get out of hand and a car was overturned. Unfortunately it is owned by a local TV rental company who have threatened to stop all credit to striking miners. At least they won't have to watch the shit being poured out constantly about the return to work!

A Deputy's car was also covered in paint because its owner has been particularly outspoken against us. He has already been bleating to the local media, and has hung a sign on his car naming the NUM as the 'hooligans' responsible. No doubt his action will result in further abuse, but whatever he suffers it will not be a fraction of what we have suffered for the past 11 months!

The *Shields Gazette* had a field day in tonight's edition, calling us 'hooligans and thugs', and reserving special indignation to report the 'horrific experience of their innocent reporter'. As innocent as Robert Maxwell or Rupert Murdoch! The sooner this nasty, tatty little rag goes bankrupt the better for the people of South Shields!

The Tories are going for the kill, announcing the closure of Frances Colliery in Scotland with the loss of 500 jobs, with more to go if the strike continues.

Thursday February 7th, 1985

I travelled up to Scotland yesterday with Fred Taylor and spent the night at Willie and Marlene Forsyth's house in Penicuik. It was great to see them again but very sad to hear that Willie has been sacked. He is very worried because he's certain the strike is going to be sold out. I agree with him but still feel confident that no deal will be signed without all the sacked miners being reinstated. We can't betray these men who have fought so hard to win the strike, or the lads who gave their lives and the lads in jail. It's unthinkable.

I spent the whole of today in the Sheriff's Court waiting to be dealt with for my arrest at Bilston Glen on July 25th! It never happened because the bastards have adjourned it yet again until March 7th! Justice my arse! The three lads who did get dealt with were all found guilty, one of them getting a £150 fine and the other two got £75 fines, with only 8 weeks to pay! One of the lads was John Scott from Westoe, and unfortunately for him his witness gave evidence that contradicted his. Another wasted journey for me.

Monday February 11th, 1985

I finally cracked today and had a huge row with Kath. I've decided to leave as soon as my case is over up in Scotland. I just can't take the hostile atmosphere any more so I've moved back to Paul McGarr's settee in Newcastle. The girls were really upset and it's not fair that we allow our hatred of each other to affect them any longer.

I spoke to a group of students at Sunderland Poly today but I was not my usual defiant self. Still, it was good to see we still have some supporters left.

Wednesday February 13th, 1985

Coal stocks were moved from Thurston and Silverwood collieries today with very little resistance. This really is the end now and I am at rock bottom.

Tomorrow should be our 13th wedding anniversary. Unlucky for us both!

Friday February 22nd, 1985

I've been so involved in talking with Kath about our split that I haven't been bothered to write. There's nothing to write about anyway; it's just doom and gloom. Ironically, Kath and me have talked more these past few days than we have in the whole of our marriage, which says everything really. I'm just waiting for the end to happen.

Tuesday February 26th, 1985

I handed in my two weeks notice to quit at the pit today. It wasn't hard but it has left me feeling terribly guilty and depressed for giving up a job I fought so hard to keep. Bloody pathetic really, but I felt it was time I put myself first for once. My marriage is well and truly on the rocks, though strangely Kath and me are getting on better than we have done for years. I am leaving for London after my final court appearance in Scotland next week. I had to hand my notice in so I can get some cash before I leave to keep me going until I can get my dole sorted out. Dole not Coal.

My guilt is lessened by the fact that the strike is lost and will almost certainly end in the next couple of weeks. Everyone seems to think it is better to go back united than risk more men becoming scabs. One lad last week, who I have stood side by side with since day one, came to the kitchen, had his dinner, and then went back to work! If things are that bad then perhaps we should make the best of it and go back with heads held high and dignity intact. I'm down but not quite out!

Monday March 4th, 1985

I attended my last picket of the longest national strike in modern times. I almost lost my voice hurling abuse at the scab buses going in. Its them bastards I blame.

Yesterday a Special Delegate Conference voted 98 to 91 for an organised return to work, with no conditions. The bastards have bowed down too far and betrayed the 600 men sacked during the strike. I'm ashamed of them!

At a mass meeting in the Armstrong Hall the Lodge officials ran true to form and merely informed the men to phone the pit to find out what shift to return on. They brushed aside complaints from men who've already phoned and been told to return to work at 10pm, night shift. The bastards are really rubbing it in because it's just over a year since we defeated the manager's plans to force all men to do night shift instead of volunteers.

Our cowardly officials are back to being compromise specialists. I really hope the lads get rid of them all at the earliest opportunity!

Tuesday March 5th, 1985

This morning I applauded as the lads marched proudly back to work behind the Lodge Banner, heads held high. They were followed by the scabs in their mobile rat cage and I had a last angry shout as they sped in.

I went into the pit to the changing rooms and collected my few belongings from my locker. I felt elated and depressed. Elated because I know I will never have to go down the pit again, and depressed because we have lost and I won't be around to rebuild the union around the young militant lads who came to the fore during the strike.

In Northumberland the men of Bates Colliery were refused entry to the pit because they were late! That's just twisting the knife. Kent have refused to go back in protest against the betrayal of the sacked men. Good for them! It's what we all should have done!

Thursday March 7th, 1985

This morning I played out my final part in the 1984-5 miners' strike when I appeared at Edinburgh Sheriff's Court to answer my 'Breach of the Peace' charge, outstanding since July. The two arresting officers both gave opposing accounts of my arrest, yet I was found guilty as charged and fined £80 with 8 weeks to pay.

So that's it, all over and done with, the most exciting, frightening and eventful year of my life so far, and one I will never, ever forget. If I was given my time over I would do it all over again.

On Saturday I leave for a new start in London and who knows what the future holds? I've given up my job, seen my marriage end, and been beaten black and blue and thrown in jail but I'd do it all again because the issues at stake were too important to do any other. One thing I am certain of, and that is the Tories won't stop here, so all those unions who stabbed us in the back better watch out because it'll be their turn next.

CHRONOLOGY

1 MARCH 1984: National Coal Board (NCB) announce the closure of Cortonwood Colliery in Yorkshire and plans for 20,000 job losses over the forthcoming year.
5 MARCH 1984: Strike starts in Yorkshire in protest, following an overwhelming vote in a ballot to take industrial action to protect jobs in the event of pit closures.
6 MARCH 1984: Scottish and Yorkshire Areas of the NUM call strike action. By 12th March half of all miners join the strike.
14 MARCH 1984: 8,000 extra police drafted into Nottinghamshire. A court rules that Yorkshire NUM must withdraw its flying pickets.
15 MARCH 1984: 23 year old miner, David Jones, killed while picketing in Ollerton, Nottinghamshire.
19 MARCH 1984: Yorkshire NUM found to be in contempt of court for not stopping pickets. NUM members picket 27 Nottinghamshire pits and peacefully persuade their colleagues to join the strike action. Police blockade Nottinghamshire.
29 MARCH 1984: Transport unions impose ban on the movement of coal, partially successfully. Nurses join the picket lines in South Wales.
5 APRIL: Nottinghamshire miners vote three to one to remain at work.
11 APRIL 1984: Pit Deputies vote to join strike, but not with necessary two-thirds majority.
19 APRIL 1984: NUM Special Conference ratifies the strike action taken by the union's areas and calls on all miners to rally to the defence of their industry.
20 APRIL 1984: Nottinghamshire and Midlands NUM decide to join strike.
2 MAY 1984: Official figures show an increase in oil use at power stations to offset coal shortage. Didcot and Aberthaw power stations shut down two days later.
23 MAY 1984: NCB walks out of talks with NUM after demanding union co-operation in the closing of 'uneconomic pits'.
25 MAY 1984: Full-scale picketing begins at the Orgreave coke works.
29 MAY 1984: Approximately 2,000 police use riot gear, horses and baton

charges to take lorries through picket lines into the Orgreave coke plant, even though workers at the plant join the miners' picket line.

31 MAY 1984: Some 3,200 police in riot gear from 13 separate police forces attack miners' pickets at Orgreave.

7 JUNE 1984: House of Commons debates miners' strike. Thousands march to lobby Parliament. 100 arrested.

15 JUNE 1984: Joe Green, miner, crushed to death on picket duty at Ferry Bridge power station.

18 JUNE 1984: The battle of Orgreave. Police run amok, 93 arrests, many miners injured including Arthur Scargill.

6 JULY 1984: NCB management begin visiting individual miners at home to encourage them to return to work.

8 JULY 1984: High Court declares NUM Annual Conference unlawful. National dock strike called against the movement of coal.

19 JULY 1984: NUM and NCB talk for 3 days. Discussion breaks down when government orders NCB not to compromise.

31 JULY 1984: South Wales NUM fined £50,000 under Tory anti-trade union legislation on picketing.

16 AUGUST 1984: South Wales NUM found in contempt of court for refusing to its pay fine. Some £770,000 of union funds seized.

23 AUGUST 1984: Ian MacGregor offers working miners 5.2% pay increase (the NUM's original pay claim) if they agree to work overtime.

24 AUGUST 1984: Second dock strike called following the unloading of coal at Hunterstone.

3 SEPTEMBER 1984: TUC meets in Brighton and votes to support miners. Support never materialises.

12 SEPTEMBER 1984: TUC attempts to organise talks between the NUM and the NCB. NACODS, the Pit Deputies' union, ballot to strike over instructions to cross picket lines.

18 SEPTEMBER 1984: Three-week dock strike called off.

26 SEPTEMBER 1984: NCB offers NACODS compromise package.

28 SEPTEMBER 1984: High Court rules that NUM cannot be forced to hold national ballot. NACODS ballot result announced–82.5% majority for strike.

29 SEPTEMBER 1984: NCB and NUM agree to talks.

1 OCTOBER 1984: Arthur Scargill is served with a High Court writ whilst sitting with the NUM delegation at the Labour Party conference. NUM executive reaffirm that the strike is official, despite the High Court ruling.

2 OCTOBER 1984: Members of the rail unions sent home for refusing to move coal.

4 OCTOBER 1984: High Court gives NUM 5 days to call off the strike.

10 OCTOBER 1984: NUM fined £200,000 and found in contempt of High Court.
11 OCTOBER 1984: NUM and NCB meet at conciliation service ACAS for talks, although Ian MacGregor tells the media 'This place stinks'.
15 OCTOBER 1984: NUM accepts two formulas put forward by ACAS. NCB walks out of talks.
17 OCTOBER 1984: NACODS calls strike for 25th October.
25 OCTOBER 1984: ACAS prepare formula which both NACODS and NUM accept. Despite TUC advice NACODS call off strike. Courts attempt to seize £200,000 of NUM funds.
26 OCTOBER 1984: High Court orders seizure of all NUM funds.
28 OCTOBER 1984: Court moves to makes 24 members of the NUM executive personally liable for the £200,000 contempt fine.
1 NOVEMBER 1984: MacGregor says: 'There is no basis for further talks with the NUM'.
4 NOVEMBER 1984: Court appointed sequestrator freezes NUM funds deposited in Ireland.
5 NOVEMBER 1984: High Court action to remove Yorkshire Area NUM officers from control over their funds.
7 NOVEMBER 1984: NUM resists sequestrator's application to return union assets to UK. Dublin Court rules £2.75 million NUM funds remain frozen and not given to sequestrator.
11 NOVEMBER 1984: NCB offers £650 Christmas bonus to striking miners who return to work by 19th November.
17 NOVEMBER 1984: NCB refuses to negotiate unless NUM gives agreement to close pits.
21 NOVEMBER 1984: Government increases deduction of supplementary benefits to £16 per week for strikers' families.
30 NOVEMBER 1984: Court appoints a receiver appointed to control NUM funds.
5 DECEMBER 1984: MacGregor announces plans to privatise pits.
9 DECEMBER 1984: Court appointed officials try to seize £4.6 million NUM funds from Luxembourg, but NUM successfully freezes the account.
22 JANUARY 1985: Court challenge to the government's right to deduct £16 from supplementary benefits paid to striking miners families fails.
24 FEBRUARY 1985: Mass rally for the miners in London—many arrests.
28 FEBRUARY 1985: MacGregor pledges that miners sacked during the strike will not be re-employed.
3 MARCH 1985: NUM ends strike. A Special Delegate Conference votes by 98-91 to return to work on 5th March 1985, without an agreement.

GLOSSARY

1972 and 1974 strikes — Two national strikes by miners against Ted Heath's Tory government. Both characterised by high levels of rank and file militancy (especially 1972). Both ended in humiliating defeats for the government.
APEX — Association of Professional, Executive, Clerical and Computer Staff. Joined GMB in 1989.
British Steel — The nationalised steel industry.
Brittan, Leon — Tory Home Secretary 1983-5.
Broad Left Organising Committee — Organised Broad Left across various unions. Tended to orientate on electing left wingers to union positions.
COSA — The white collar section of the NUM.
CP — Communist Party, whose paper is the *Morning Star*.
DHSS — Department of Health and Social Security, responsible for social security payments. Split up in 1988.
Flying pickets — When groups of workers picket workplaces other than their own.
Gandhi, Mrs — Indira Gandhi, prime minister of India. Assassinated Oct 31st 1984 in revenge for bloody repression in Punjab.
GCHQ — The government spy centre in Cheltenham where Margaret Thatcher banned trade unions in January 1984.
GMBU — The General, Municipal and Boilermakers' Union. Now GMB.
Grunwicks — A photo processing plant in West London where predominantly Asian women workers fought for union recognition. Arthur Scargill led a large delegation of miners to support their picket.
Heathfield, Peter — General secretary of the NUM during the miners strike 1984-5
Howells, Kim — South Wales NUM official. Later became Labour MP.
Incentive Scheme — The pit incentive scheme tied wages to output, so favouring areas with lower-costs like Nottinghamshire. It sowed the seed of the divisions of 1984-5. Introduced under the Labour Government of 1974-9 and backed by the then Energy Secretary Tony Benn. Miners rejected it in a secret ballot nationally, but this was ignored.
Jarrow Marchers — Unemployed marches in 1930s.
Kinnock, Neil — Leader of the Labour Party 1983 to 1992.
Lawson, Nigel — Tory Chancellor of the Exchequer 1983 to 1989.
Lodges — NUM local branches.

MacGregor, Ian — Tory-appointed head of the National Coal Board.
Maxwell, Robert — Media magnate, owner of *Daily Mirror* from July 1984. Stole pension funds.
McGahey, Mick — Scottish miners leader and Communist Party member.
Militant — Newspaper of important left wing group inside Labour Party during 1980s.
Murray, Len — General Secretary of the TUC, 1973–1984.
NACODS — The pit deputies' union, whose members were responsible for safety and acted as foremen in the pits.
NALGO — National Association of Local Government Officers. Now part of Unison
NCB — National Coal Board, the government body that ran the nationalised mining industry.
NGA — National Graphical Association, a print union. See also Warrington.
NUJ — National Union of Journalists.
NUPE — National Union of Public Employees. Later merged with other unions to form UNISON.
NUR — National Union of Railwaymen. Now part of RMT.
Pit Deputies — see NACODS.
quorum — Minimum attendance figure at a union meeting for decisions taken to be valid.
Saltley Gates — A coke depot in Birmingham that was the scene of a mass miners picket in February 1972 led by Arthur Scargill. Miners were joined by thousands of striking Birmingham engineers and the police were forced to shut the depot. A major victory and the turning point of the 1972 strike.
SDP — Social Democratic Party, a right wing split form Labour formed in 1981, later merged with Liberals to form Liberal Democrats. 'Dr Death' was the press nickname for the SDP leader, David Owen.
'Silver Birch' — Scab miner who organised working Nottingham miners.
Skinner, Dennis — Labour MP for Bolsover in Derbyshire.
Taylor, Jack — Head of Yorkshire NUM.
TGWU — Transport and General Workers Union. Now part of Unite.
Warrington — In 1983 a bitter confrontation took place at the *Stockport Messenger* in Warrington in a battle to break the power of the print unions.
WRP — Workers Revolutionary Party.